POPCORN IN PARADISE

The Wit and Wisdom of Hollywood

And there was popcorn in paradise.
(Ben M. Hall)

POPCORN IN PARADISE:

The Wit and Wisdom of Hollywood

192 ill 24cm

★★★★★★★★★★★★★★★★★

Edited by
John Robert Colombo

A Jonathan-James Book

HOLT, RINEHART AND WINSTON
New York

Acknowledgments

To the contributors to this collection, both living and dead, I am grateful, for without their words there would be no book. The off-camera remarks included in these pages come from innumerable articles, reviews, and interviews published in newspapers, magazines, journals, and books —especially autobiographical and anecdotal volumes dealing with individuals and film history. The sources are simply too numerous to acknowledge individually.

For assistance in assembling this material, I would like to record my thanks to: Michael Richardson and Philip Singer of the North York Public Library in Metropolitan Toronto; David Beard of Cine Books, Toronto and Vancouver; Gerald Pratley who, ten years ago, founded the Ontario Film Institute, located in the Ontario Science Centre, Metropolitan Toronto; Irving Frankle of Super Pufft Popcorn, Ltd., Scarborough, Ontario; Elwy Yost, long-time friend, author, and host of TVO's *Saturday Night at the Movies*; Joanna Ruderfer, a star in anybody's book; authors Nancy McPhee and Doug Fetherling; David Thompson, author of *A Biographical Dictionary of the Cinema* (1975); Roger Manvell, editor of *The International Encyclopedia of Film* (1972); the indispensable Leslie Halliwell, famous for *The Filmgoer's Companion* (Sixth Edition, 1976); Allan J. Stormont, Carolyn Brunton, and Patrick Crean of Jonathan-James Books, and especially their editor, Conrad Wieczorek, who saw in the manuscript the shape of the book to come; and, finally, Ruth Colombo, my wife and filmgoing companion.

J.R.C.

First published in the United States of America in 1980 by Holt, Rinehart and Winston, 383 Madison Avenue, New York, New York 10017.

Library of Congress Cataloging in Publication Data

Colombo, John Robert.
  Popcorn in paradise:
the wit and wisdom of Hollywood.

  "A Jonathan-James book."

  1. Moving-picture industry—United States—Quotations, maxims, etc.
2. Moving-picture producers and directors—United States—Quotations.   3. Moving-picture actors and actresses—United States—Quotations.   4. Moving-picture industry—United States—Anecdotes, facetiae, satire, etc.   I. Colombo, John Robert, 1936-

PN1993.5.U6P58   791.43'0973

79-22186

ISBN 0-03-056144-2

Jonathan-James Books
5 Sultan Street
Toronto, Ontario
Canada M5S 1L6

Edited by Conrad Wieczorek
Illustrations by Graham Pilsworth
Designed by Jack Steiner

First American Edition

Printed in the United States of America
10 9 8 7 6 5 4 3 2 1

Program

POPCORN IN PARADISE

This book is for those who enjoy reading about the movies. It's also for people who appreciate "quotable quotes," offering, as it does, some three thousand remarks made by some seven hundred movie personalities through the years. The quotations were collected to entertain the film buff and to suggest that the moviemakers, being human, like the rest of us, can be as fascinating off screen as they are on screen.

The cast of characters includes the film world's leading figures: superstars, actors and actresses, supporting players, producers, directors, writers—even reviewers and critics. Screen favorites are caught, in and out of character, making personal appearances, playing cameo roles. They speak about themselves and about their lives, and, naturally, they have a lot to say about movie-making itself. Two-thirds of the quotations have to do with the *reel* world. But life presents its problems too, and so you'll find lines dealing with things that preoccupy us all at one time or another—money, sex, looks, self-esteem, careers—problems in the *real* world.

Perhaps what the stars and others have to say differs in no pronounced way from what we ourselves would say, if *our* names were household words, if *our* faces were familiar around the world, and if interviewers flocked around *us*, pen and paper in hand, tape recorders or television cameras switched on, to catch *our* passing comments and considered opinions. However, we do tend to measure their words and actions, both on and off camera, against our own in similar circumstances. This is the bond between the actor and the audience, the sympathy made possible by the producer, the director, and the technician.

This book deals with an ordinary human activity: people, in this case film-makers, talking about their work and their lives, hence, the title above combines both the silly and the sublime. The popcorn is the silly part. Popcorn was introduced to confectionary stands in moviehouses about the time the talkies came to the screen, and both have been with us ever since. The confectionary stand is the first thing the moviegoer encounters after he has bought his ticket and entered the lobby, and it's the last thing he sees when he makes his exit. Around the world, popcorn is synonymous with the movie-going experience. Perhaps the fun food is passing out of favor, with a diet-conscious viewing public, or a clientele that goes to art cinemas rather than first-run movie houses, but the day when it dies out has not yet dawned. To some, the puffed-up grain symbolizes the worst aspects of Hollywood, something tawdry, something synthetic, "popcorn venus," and so on. But to the vast movie-going public, the aroma of freshly popped corn, salted and gooey with melted butter, is a nourishing and indispensable part of the excitement of the movies.

So much for the silliness. Just as each popped corn comes out of a kernel, popcorn is symbolic of the illusions that are hatched on the screen: the happy endings, the typecasting, and so on. But where illusions abound, so do ideals, and these may be symbolized by the word paradise in my title. The English word "paradise" comes from the Persian word for "park" or "pleasure ground," a notion not too many removes from the technological "pleasure dome" of the motion-picture palace of the past. Paradise is a place of vision, where our deep-seated needs are satisfied. The moviehouse attempts to gratify these needs too, but in a vicarious manner, by showing us things we might not normally see. "Paradise has palm trees," Hildegarde Knef says elsewhere in this book. And so does Hollywood.

By linking "popcorn" and "paradise" together, this book suggests that life is a mix of the ephemeral and the eternal, and it implies that our survival depends on both handfuls of popcorn and visions of paradise. Both are necessary, but in the proper proportion. Taken together, the two of them, balanced and blended, in amounts different for each person, they make for happiness, well being, and a good life.

Moviemakers, more than most people, are concerned with such contrasts: with reconciling the irreconcilables of life, commerce and art, and of finding an aesthetically pleasing balance in the world around us. Who better can relate the illusory and the ideal, the gaudy and the good, the trivia and the treasure—with poise? The motion-picture projector shows us, larger than life, our hopes and fears, our follies and philosophies, our aspirins and aspirations, in sound and in color. In "living color," as they say.

On the whole, I've let the stars and others speak for themselves, with minimal direction from me. After all, since 1927, talking has been a big part of their business. The result is that the quotations, even the simple ones, glow. If you or I say, "I love no one," the meaning of the remark and its emotional value are circumscribed by the people you and I know. But if Greta Garbo says it, and she did say it, off camera, it takes on the aura of memorability. The remark is seen as Sibylline, is heard as Delphic. "I love no one" seems a curse, a larger-than-life tragedy, the Greek *hamartia* (or "fatal flaw"), perhaps. So the stars speak for themselves. Occasionally I have let others speak about them, as in the "Close-ups" in "The Superstars" and elsewhere through the book, and in the "Extra Takes" in "Short Subjects"—observations made, over the years, by friends, enemies, close associates, and innocent bystanders.

The Movies

This chapter, which deals with motion pictures in general terms, is called "The Movies." I would like to have called it *The Eyes and Ears of the World*, but this is the title, copyright by Paramount News, for their popular and distinctive series of newsreels seen from 1927 to 1957.

Newsreels are now a thing of the past, relegated to film archives by the late-night news on television, five, six, or seven nights a week. In these archives, and in the air-conditioned vaults of the major film studios, rest the world's film footage. A million miles of the memory of man. Is there an aspect of life, no matter how insignificant, that has not been filmed? Is there a site somewhere on the surface of the globe that has not been photographed by a cameraman? The beauty of a flower, the movement of an animal, which has not attracted the attention of a director? Is there a human act, even the most intimate, that has not been caught in a fix of silver nitrate on celluloid, to be threaded through a projector and shown and reshown countless times? Has anyone had a thought or feeling that has not been thought or felt by an actor or actress before a camera? Is there a plot that has not been filmed countless times?

With so much film footage being exposed, it is surprising that the average person doesn't trip over reels and cannisters. Thinking such thoughts, I asked myself the following question: How many films have been made? How many movies have been produced since the invention of the Kinetoscope by Thomas A. Edison in New Jersey on October 6, 1886? While it is true the number of existing films can no more be counted than can the stars in the heavens, it is also true that imaginative astronomers frequently guess at the number of stars in the universe, so why shouldn't a film writer do the same with the movies?

The British film chronicler, Leslie Halliwell, has gone on record as estimating that 25,000 feature-length films have been produced in the English-speaking world alone from the early days to 1977. When I first read this figure, I thought some error had been made. After all, that is a lot of footage, and how many features can *you* name? But when I talked with Gerald Pratley, author and head of the Ontario Film Institute, I heard him concur with the Halliwell figure and even hazard a guess as to feature-film production in the entire world. He fixed on the number of features, both silent and sound, in all languages, as close to 100,000!.

But Pratley had more to offer. "If I had to guess, I would say that in the first century of motion-picture production there have been *two million* films. Of course, I include in this round figure all features in all languages, including silent ones, plus short features, documentaries, made-for-television movies, and all general-interest movies. Two million would be my rough estimate."

Armed with Pratley's figure, I decided to compute how long it would take a single person to watch all these films. I assume that the average film runs twenty minutes, the approximate length of a silent two-reeler (although a feature film today runs about a hundred minutes), and that an inveterate moviegoer could watch films without interruption twenty-four hours a day, 365 days a year (making no allowance for leap year), an absurd situation to be sure! Yet it would take this bleary-eyed person 788 years to watch all these two million films. If he sat down in a plush seat and was well-supplied with nourishing popcorn in 1980, he would finish in the year 2768. He would be bleary-eyed, yet he would leave untouched all the films released during those 788 years.

If that sounds so exhausting, it is as a relief that we turn to today's feature films, and also to the comments to come, which suggest not only some of the variety to be found in the domain of dreams called the movies, but also the widely differing ways in which different kinds of people understand the medium itself. This chapter, really, is only a sampler of things to come. Throughout the book and, especially in the chapter on writers, you'll find many of the major characters speaking about what the movies mean to them.

INVENTORS

I consider that the greatest mission of the motion picture is first to make people happy. . .to bring more joy and cheer and wholesome good will into this world of ours. And God knows we need it.
— Thomas A. Edison

Young man, you should be grateful, since, although my invention is not for sale, it would undoubtedly ruin you. It can be exploited for a certain time as a scientific curiosity, but, apart from that, it has no commercial future whatsoever. — Auguste Lumière

ACTORS

The movies are the only business where you can go out front and applaud yourself. — Will Rogers

I started out in vaudeville, and vaudeville died. I hit the burlesque houses, and they padlocked 'em. I tried radio, and you know what happened to radio. Then live TV, and it vanished. Now that I've finally got a toehold in movies, look what's happening to them.
— Jack Albertson

PIONEER PRODUCER

I always bragged of the fact that no second of those contained in the twenty-four hours ever passed but that the name of William Fox was on the screen, being exhibited in some theater in some part of the world. — William Fox

DIRECTORS

Cinema should make you forget you are sitting in the theater.
— Roman Polanski

What I find most encouraging in recent years—and I am speaking of Europe—is the fact that the public no longer simply "goes to the movies," but goes to see a particular film. — René Clement

Not making the films you should be making is awful, but making them and not having them shown is worse. — Claude Jutra

I think that the French cinema is in the process of dying. Under the excess of so-called intellectualism on the one hand, and the excess of vulgarity on the other. — Julien Duvivier

The camera is a little bit like the knife of a surgeon. — Jean Renoir

The eye hears, the ear sees. — Norman McLaren

In cinema, we must select everything for the camera according to the richness of its power to reveal. — Satyajit Ray

The cinema must become scientific; it must learn to dispense knowledge and consciousness. — Roberto Rossellini

The basic aim of cinema is to teach men to see all things new, to abandon the commonplace world in which they blindly live, and to discover, at last, the meaning and beauty of the universe.
— V.I. Pudovkin

Kinodrama is an opium for the people. — Dziga Vertov

SCREENWRITERS

Making movies is a game played by a few thousand toy-minded folk. — Ben Hecht

We have multitudes of sleeping beings inside us, and imagined experiences projected on the screen enable these wraiths within us to wake up and live lives—and so make us larger people.
— Dudley Nichols

People needed a dream world to get away from the awfulness of the reality around them—breadlines and all that. And boy, did we know how to give them dreams! — Donald Ogden Stewart

WRITERS

The phenomena on the screen are the phenomena of the soul.
— Carl Hauptman

Because of capitalism's astonishing prostitution of the cinema, we are confronted by a vast mountain of films, which must surely be the greatest collection of rubbish of our time.— Marguerite Duras

Its trade, which is in dreams at so many dollars per thousand feet, is managed by businessmen pretending to be artists and by artists pretending to be businessmen. In this queer atmosphere, nobody stays as he was; the artist begins to lose his art, and the businessman becomes temperamental and overbalanced.— J.B. Priestley

Movies won't be an art until the materials are as inexpensive as paper and pencil.— Jean Cocteau

Edison is the new Gutenberg. He has invented the new printing. The state that realizes this may lead the soul of America, day after tomorrow.— Vachel Lindsay

STATESMAN

When the spirit of the people is lower than at any other time during this depression, it is a splendid thing that for just fifteen cents an American can go to a movie and look at the smiling face of a baby and forget his troubles. — Franklin Delano Roosevelt

CRIME FIGHTER

I have personally viewed several of these "Crime Does Not Pay" pictures and feel that they are performing a most worthwhile purpose in helping to curb crime.— J. Edgar Hoover

PROPAGANDA MINISTER

What a good idea of mine it was to have taken possession of the film industry on behalf of the Reich several years ago!— Joseph Goebbels

COMMUNIST LEADERS

The cinema is for us the most important instrument of all the arts.— Nikolai Lenin

The cinema in the hands of the Soviet power represents a great and priceless force.— Joseph Stalin

Cinema was and remains one of the major battlefields of the ideological struggle raging in the world today.— Nikolai V. Podgorny

OTHER EYES

You see people naked through the viewfinder. — Henri Cartier-Bresson

It is the movies, and only the movies, that do justice to that material-istic interpretation of the universe which, whether we like it or not, pervades contemporary civilization. — Erwin Panofsky

The Chinese call movies "Electric Shadows." — Jonas Mekas

The coming of the Motion Picture was as important as that of the Printing Press. — William Randolph Hearst

I believe that motion pictures are the most vital influence upon public thought in the world today. — Adele Rogers St. Johns

On the spiritual plane, the cinema is an invention every whit as impor-tant as, on the material plane, the freeing of nuclear energy.
— Jean Debrix

2
Hollywood!

Sunset Boulevard, Grauman's Chinese Theatre, Beverly Hills, Schwab's Drug Store, Malibu, Hollywood and Vine, Brown Derby, Wilshire Boulevard, Garden of Allah, Griffith Park, San Simeon, Chateau Marmont, Hollywood Bowl, Disneyland. . . .

How many have I missed? How many of the famous landmarks of Hollywood and the Hollywoodites have been left out? Hollywood, the world's best-known suburb! These place names are etched in the memories of countless millions of moviegoers who have not only never been to Hollywood but have no intention of ever visiting the fabled place.

Today, with studio tours, one can even "Sleep Where Liz Taylor Slept!" (Sheraton Town House), but the glamor has leaked away, and the studios created by immigrant pioneers ("pants-pressers," Joseph Kennedy, one-time studio executive and father of JFK, called them)—Warner's, Twentieth-Century Fox, Paramount, Universal, Columbia, Metro-Goldwyn-Mayor—have changed beyond recognition, producing for television, gobbled up by conglomerates, or former talent agents concerned with tax shelters and write-offs and spin-offs and commercial tie-ins. Some say that the studio-system of the Thirties and Forties was immoral, but scarcely anyone has a good word to say about the production styles of the Sixties and Seventies.

Still, films of quality *are* produced. Today's "Hollywood" film, however, though it may bear the monogram of a major studio still located in Hollywood, was probably financed in Tokyo, shot near Cairo, and edited outside London. Today's film is supposed to be tomorrow's fashion, but it's unlikely the stars and producers and directors will ever again influence the manners of others, to the extent recalled by Anita Loos:

> *I remember when stars had to put on black glasses because of the Hollywood sun, and suddenly black glasses became the rage all over the world. And they're still worn by people who don't need them; that is, they don't need them for protection from the sun.*
> *Fade out the new Hollywood, fade in the old Hollywood.*

As film writer Alex Barris sees it:

> *Hollywood's future still seemed to be in its past. Audiences still seemed eager to be shown again and told again what a glamorous, nutty, greedy, corrupt, decadent, irresistible place Hollywood was. . . and maybe still is.*

13

In the words of the song from *Hollywood Hotel* (1937), sung by Johnny Davis and Frances Langford, with Benny Goodman and his orchestra (words by Johnny Mercer, music by Richard Whiting):

> *Hooray for Hollywood,*
> *That screwy, ballyhooey Hollywood....*

So here are a hundred or so observations on Hollywood, made by those who know her (if Hollywood is a she) well, along with a few people who were just "passing through." Some observers, like Fred Allen and F. Scott Fitzgerald, are both for and against the place. If the "Pros" are fewer than the "cons"—there are only 31 contributors who actually approve of Hollywood to 49 who are on record disapproving—the moral to be derived is not that Hollywood is a bad place but that it is a fascinatingly bad place, another matter entirely!

HOLLYWOOD?—YES!

California is a great place—if you happen to be an orange. Hollywood is a place where people from Iowa mistake each other for stars.— Fred Allen

The most wonderful accident that ever happened to me was my coming out to this God-given, vital, youthful, sunny place.
—John Barrymore

What I like about Hollywood is that one can get along by knowing two words of English—swell and lousy.— Vicki Baum

To go to California and not see Hollywood is like going to Ireland and not seeing the Lakes of Killarney.— Brendan Behan

Hollywood is like Picasso's bedroom.— Candice Bergen

I won't hear a word against Hollywood. Hollywood means to me cash, courage, and climate.— Mrs. Patrick Campbell

And if there was ever a world of chance—that world was Hollywood.— Lenore Coffee

...the only big city in the States without a railway station, by the way.— Austin J. Cross

Hollywood...the most sensational merry-go-round ever built.
—Tony Curtis

It is a sobering thought that the decisions we make at our desks in Hollywood may intimately affect the lives of human beings, men, women and children, throughout the world.— Cecil B. DeMille

California, you see, was a dream.— Geraldine Farrar

Suffice to summarize. I have been to Hollywood—talked with Taylor, dined with March, danced with Ginger Rogers (this will burn Scottie up, but it's true), been in Rosalind Russell's drawing room, wisecracked with Montgomery, drunk (ginger ale) with Zukor and Lasky, lunched alone with Maureen O'Sullivan, watched Crawford act, and lost my heart to a beautiful half-caste Chinese girl whose name I've forgotten. — F. Scott Fitzgerald

The very narcissism of Hollywood becomes part of its charm.
— Robert Fulford

Hollywood is now a place to retire to. — Paulette Goddard

The ocean is here, as beautiful as the Metropolitan Museum of Art. — Lee Grant

I believe that God felt sorry for actors, so He created Hollywood to give them a place in the sun and a swimming pool. — Sir Cedric Hardwicke

There'll always be an England . . . even if it's in Hollywood. — Bob Hope

Hollywood really was "the city of beautiful nonsense" in the Twenties. — Leatrice Joy

For Hollywood is no longer a geographical entity or, as some would have it, a state of mind: It is that golden, almost mythic place in the West where the movies come from. — Arthur Knight

Hollywood . . . the place where there is assembled the greatest number of creative people in the entire world. — Stanley Kramer

It wasn't good to take the soft lights off the tinsel. — Jerry Lewis

Will this land furthest west be the first to capture the inner spirit of this newest and most curious of the arts? — Vachel Lindsay

There isn't another spot on earth, where I could obtain one-tenth the mental, moral, spiritual, and aesthetic joy that I get right here!
— Anita Loos

Immorality? Oh, my God! Hollywood seemed to me to be one of the most respectable towns in America. Even Baltimore can't beat it. — Aimee Semple McPherson

Hollywood is a sewer—with service from the Ritz-Carlton.
— Wilson Mizner

I like it here. It's like living on the moon, isn't it? When I first came here they told me, "You'll be so bored you'll die; nobody talks about anything but pictures." After I was here a week, I discovered I didn't want to talk about anything else myself. — Cole Porter

Beverly Hills, by the way, is the only place in the world where the police have an unlisted telephone number. — Rex Reed

A bewildering place, Hollywood! There are enough unwritten true-life stories right on the lots to make exciting plots for innumerable pictures for years to come. — Lowell Thomas

To love Hollywood, as I do, is to love something in spite of itself. . . . But the awfulness of Hollywood, in every sense of the word, is ultimately more absorbing in its sometimes pathetic, and often

terrifying way, than the "glamorous" myth still feebly perpetuated by the picture postcards. — Edward Thorpe

I love Los Angeles. I love Hollywood. They're beautiful. Everybody's plastic. I want to be plastic. — Andy Warhol

Hollywood is a very quiet place. . . . very quiet. . . . No drinking—very little smoking. And as for the evenings. . .they're practically inaudible. No sound at all but the popping of the California poppies.
— Adolph Zukor

HOLLYWOOD?—NO!

You can take all the sincerity in Hollywood, place it in the navel of a fruit fly and still have room enough for three caraway seeds and a producer's heart. — Fred Allen

I like to work in Hollywood, but I don't like to live there. I'm too young to die. — Claire Bloom

To survive in Hollywood you need: the ambition of a Latin-American revolutionary; the ego of a grand opera tenor; and the physical stamina of a cow pony. — Billie Burke

There is one word which describes Hollywood. It is: "Nervous."
— Frank Capra

Los Angeles is a city with the personality of a paper cup.
— Raymond Chandler

In 1940, I had my choice between Hitler and Hollywood, and I preferred Hollywood. Just a little. — René Clair

Hollywood is no place for a woman to find a husband, especially her own. — Denise Darcel

The old Hollywood was a kind of tinsel cocoon, from which emerged so many gorgeous butterflies, glittering creatures that flew high and fast. . .then too often fluttered earthwards, wings broken.
— Lotta Dempsey

. . .the only place in the world where a man can get stabbed in the back while climbing a ladder. — William Faulkner

You can take Hollywood for granted as I did, or you can dismiss it with the contempt we reserve for what we don't understand. It can be understood too, but only dimly and in flashes. — F. Scott Fitzgerald

It was a strange world. I had the feeling I was living during the last days of Pompeii. — Geraldine Fitzgerald

They've great respect for the dead in Hollywood—but none for the living. — Errol Flynn

Hollywood is a place where your best friend will plunge a knife in your back and then call the police to tell them that you are carrying a concealed weapon. — George Frazier

Hollywood has never had a shortage of the sort of person who, in the midst of a burning house, will sit down to write a speech explaining how he, personally, always chose non-combustible materials when they were reasonably priced and acceptable to his associates.
— Robert Fulford

...an emotional Detroit. — Lillian Gish

...a world of dwarfs casting long shadows. — Sheila Graham

California was sunning itself on the beaches, and Hollywood was behind me, the city of unreality, stardust, and people's dreams.
— John Grierson

It is the dullest place in the world, the empty studios with their depleted back lots retaining no trace of the glory that shone around Ernst Lubitsch, James Whale and Preston Sturges. Luckily the films live on, in one form or another. — Leslie Halliwell

Hollywood may be thickly populated, but to me it's still a bewilderness. — Sir Cedric Hardwicke

...the most boss-ridden town in the world. — Ben Hecht

Hollywood is the world's most beautiful set and the lousiest scenario.
— Harry Hirschfield

In Hollywood, gratitude is Public Enemy Number One. — Hedda Hopper

Get out of that fake Hollywood atmosphere into life that is real, ghastly, forbidding, and magnificent. — Elsie Janis

Hollywood...where everyone's a genius until he's lost his job.
— Erskine Johnson

...where there is no definition of your worth earlier than your last picture. — Murray Kempton

Hollywood today is less the place where films are made than where films are made from. — Arthur Knight

If I ever wrote a book about Hollywood and its inner workings, I know what I would call it—Insincere City. — Mervyn LeRoy

Strip away the phony tinsel of Hollywood and you find the real tinsel underneath. — Oscar Levant

A leader of public thought in Hollywood wouldn't have sufficient mental acumen anywhere else to hold down a place in the bread line! — Anita Loos

It would not have been possible to have Hollywood in Chicago: they are having a nineteenth century. — Marshall McLuhan

Just outside Los Angeles is Hollywood, a colony of picture stars. Its morals are those of Port Said. — H.L. Mencken

Hollywood is a carnival where there are no concessions.

17

I thought it was going to be like a delightful trip through a sewer in a glass-bottomed boat. — Wilson Mizner

...a place where they'll pay you ten thousand dollars for a kiss and fifty cents for your soul. — Marilyn Monroe

...where you spend more than you make, on things you don't need, to impress people you don't like. — Ken Murray

Hollywood impresses me as being ten million dollars' worth of intricate and highly ingenious machinery functioning elaborately to put skin on baloney. — George Jean Nathan

Hollywood...the land of yes-men and acqui-yes girls.

If all those sweet young things present were laid end to end, I wouldn't be at all surprised. — Dorothy Parker

Hollywood is a cruel place—relentless, stern, and unforgiving—as I suppose all great industrial centers must be. — Basil Rathbone

In Hollywood, if you don't have happiness, you send out for it.
                                                        — Rex Reed

Not long ago the famous sign that dominates the hills overlooking Hollywood dropped an O—quite an irony for a town whose livelihood depends on keeping up appearances. — Glenys Roberts

In a capital of atheism like Hollywood, what can a man believe in?
                                                        — Joseph M. Schenck

Hollywood's like Egypt, full of crumbled pyramids. It'll never come back. It'll just keep on crumbling until finally the wind blows the last studio props across the sands. — David O. Selznick

Hollywood stands in the way of much that film might be.
                                                        — Charles Siepmann

Above all, Hollywood is a community of lonely people searching for even the most basic kind of stimulation in their otherwise mundane lives. — Rod Steiger

The only way to avoid Hollywood is to live there. — Igor Stravinsky

Standing in the midst of a gay Hollywood party the other evening, an ancient Oriental proverb that goes like this flashed through my mind, "Dignity begins where boasting ends." — Cornelius Vanderbilt, Jr.

This is the only town where you can say, "Come up and see me some time," and not get taken up on it. — Mae West

I never stayed longer than six weeks....Corruption begins on the morning of the seventh week. — Thornton Wilder

Hollywood is a town where they place you under contract instead of observation.

...a place where they shoot too many pictures and not enough actors. — Walter Winchell

The Superstars

What does Chaplin have in common with Tracy, Garbo with Garland, Brando with Grant? Some are fine actors; others are not. Some are versatile and can play many roles; others (as the saying goes) play only themselves. But what they do have in common is star quality, an indefinable but ever-present "something extra" that distinguishes them from "the players." These are the superstars, the stars who were legends in their own time, and are legends in our time as well. Each one's name could be placed above the title.

TALLULAH BANKHEAD

Tallulah Bankhead (1902-1968) was the toast of both West End and Broadway stages, and, while she turned in some fine film performances, she never did find her niche in Hollywood. Her better pictures include: *Tarnished Lady* (1931), *Lifeboat* (1944), *A Royal Scandal* (1945), and *Die Die My Darling* (1965). Having heard it once, who could ever forget her gravel-voiced drawl?

This great lady of the stage, once said:

> *Nobody can be exactly like me. Sometimes even I have trouble doing it.*

She had a thing about stage and screen credits:

> *I've lived for too long, stage center, to submit to second billing.*

About a part she once refused to play she said:

> *There is less in this than meets the eye.*

Sex was sometimes on her mind:

> *It's the good girls who keep diaries; the bad girls never have the time.*

And:

> *I'm a single-standard girl. I found no surprises in the Kinsey Report.*

(One wonders what the "single-standard" was!) About food and drink and other forms of nourishment, she was eloquent:

Daddy warned me about drinking and men, but he never said anything about women and drugs.

I've had six juleps, and I'm not even sober.

When I was sixteen, dahling, I had a shoebox full of cocaine.

Tallulah could, however, be serious when she wanted. Witness these lines about life:

The only thing I regret about my past is the length of it. If I had to live my life again I'd make all the same mistakes—only sooner.

My philosophy is best expressed by a vagrant line from some book or play: We're all paid off in the end, and the fools first.

CLOSE-UPS

Miss Bankhead isn't well enough known nationally to warrant my imitating her. — Bette Davis

A day away from Tallulah is like a month in the country.
— Howard Dietz

Tallulah who?— Beatrice Lillie

THE BARRYMORES

There are three major and two minor Barrymores, certainly enough for any two generations of actors and actresses!

The oldest was Lionel (1878-1954), a hard-working film star and director, somewhat humorless too, who appeared in fifteen films as Dr. Gillespie, well-loved family physician. Lionel is best remembered today for his parts in *Grand Hotel* (1932), *Treasure Island* (1934), *Camille* (1936), and *You Can't Take It With You* (1938).

The revered Ethel (1879-1959) specialized in playing regal (then crotchety) ladies on Broadway and in Hollywood. She had a grand, weepy manner about her and may be seen to good effect in *None But The Lonely Heart* (1944), *The Farmer's Daughter* (1947), *Kind Lady* (1951), and *Deadline* (1952).

The youngest of the first-generation Barrymores—and the most famous— was John (1882-1942), billed as "The Great Lover" or "The Great Profile." He played a romantic Hamlet on the Broadway stage but took to drink, and in the movies he squandered his talent and drank even more heavily. He played a ham actor-manager in *Twentieth Century* (1934) and an aging lover in *Grand Hotel* (1932).

John's two children, Diana (1921-60) and John Barrymore Jr. (born 1932), were stage-struck too. Diana appeared in *Between Us Girls* (1942) and *Ladies Courageous* (1944). John Jr. has appeared in *The Sundowners* (1950) and *War of the Zombies* (1963).

The Barrymores were stagey, even somewhat stodgy. Yet, for a time, they were regarded as "the first family of film."

Lionel, at the best of times, was simply not very quotable. Late in his career he complained to a producer:

Look, son, I'm seventy-five years old—nothing is as much fun as it used to be.

And he had this to say about his younger brother John:

It takes an earthquake to get Jack out of bed, a flood to make him wash, and the United States Army to put him to work.

John was talkative, garrulous some might say. He had opinions on everything, especially sex:

The trouble with life is that there are so many beautiful women—and so little time.

Aging was a difficult thing to accept:

I'm fifty years old, and I want to look like Jackie Cooper's grandson.

He had a number of unhappy love affairs:

A paper napkin never returns from a laundry—nor love from a trip to the law courts.

Theories of acting, bah!

Method acting? There are quite a few methods. Mine involves a lot of talent, a glass, and some cracked ice.

On his daughter Diana:

Diana is a horse's arse, quite a pretty one, but still a horse's arse.

But he had presence, even if preposterously expressed at times:

My head is buried in the sands of tomorrow, while my tail-feathers are singed by the hot sun of today.

Ethel knew her limitations and strengths and loved her calling:

For an actress to be a success, she must have the face of Venus, the brains of Minerva, the grace of Terpsichore, the memory of Macaulay, the figure of Juno, and the hide of a rhinoceros.

She had no illusions about the immortality of thespians:

We who play, who entertain for a few years, what can we leave that will last?

And could be counted upon to come out in favor of common sense:

You grow up the day you have your first real laugh at yourself.

CLOSE-UPS

The Happy Family.— Alma Power-Waters

That's all there is. There isn't any more. . . . . —Ethel Barrymore's familiar line in the play *Sunday.*

HUMPHREY BOGART & LAUREN BACALL

The Sixties conferred cult status on Humphrey Bogart (1899-1957) and his widow Lauren Bacall (born 1924), career-minded stage and screen stars both. His image remains as bright as ever in such films as *The Petrified Forest* (1936), *The Maltese Falcon* (1941) in which he played Sam Spade (considered by some to be the "quintessential" Bogart), *Casablanca* (1943), *The Treasure of the Sierra Madre* (1948), *The African Queen* (1952), and *The Caine Mutiny* (1954). With Bacall, he starred in *To Have and Have Not* (1944), *The Big Sleep* (1946), *Dark Passage* (1947), and *Key Largo* (1948). She returned to Broadway (with *Cactus Flower*), and her later films include *Harper* (1966) and *Murder on the Orient Express* (1974). Bogart and Bacall go together like—well, theirs was an interesting relationship.

Bogart fascinates, perhaps because his approach to his role was simple and cool:

> *All you owe the public is a good performance.*

He knew the value of stardom—dollars:

> *To be a star you have to drag your weight into the box office and be recognized wherever you go.*

> *What makes me think I'm worth $250,000 a picture? Because I can get it.*

BOGART
1941

> *The only reason to make a million dollars in this business is to tell some fat producer to go to hell.*

Drinking was more than relaxing; it seemed to have something to do with being a man:

> *The trouble with the world is that everybody in it is three drinks behind.*

> *I don't trust any bastard who doesn't drink. People who don't drink are afraid of revealing themselves.*

It is said his last words were:

> *I never should have switched from Scotch to Martinis.*

Bacall was Bogey's buddy as well as a personality in her own right.

> *I'm not a member of the weaker sex.*

About love and affection, she said:

> *Invisible chains last longer.*

> *I hope my daughter will know that the passion of anger is also a part of love and that the opposite of love is not hate—but indifference.*

She reminisced about Bogey's Rat Pack:

> *You had to stay up late and get drunk, and all our members were against the PTA.*

Nostalgia means looking backward and not forward:

> *Sometimes I've thought that if the public didn't stop taking those trips down Memory Lane about me, I was going to lose my mind. . . being a widow isn't exactly a profession.*

About her career as a star in her own right:

> *I'm due. I'm overdue.*

CLOSE-UPS.

Bogart can be tough without a gun.
Like Edward G. Robinson, all Bogart has to do to dominate a scene is to enter it. — Raymond Chandler

Bogey's a helluva nice guy until 11:30 p.m. After that he thinks he's Bogart. — Dave Chasen

He had the damnedest façade of any man I ever met in my life. He was playing Bogart all the time, but he was really a big, sloppy bowl of mush. — Stanley Kramer

Humphrey Bogart is a first-class person with an obsessive tendency to behave like a second-class person. — Mike Romanoff

MARLON BRANDO

Brando, who was born in 1924 and lives most of the time on a South Sea island near Tahiti, must be the highest paid actor in history, commanding multi-million-dollar fees plus percentages for brief appearances. His better films include *A Streetcar Named Desire* (1951), *On the Waterfront* (1954), *The Godfather* (1972), in which he played the aging Don Corleone, and *Last Tango in Paris* (1973). More recently he appeared as the father of the Man of Steel in *Superman* (1978).

A characteristic of Brando is his pronounced views on the acting profession:

> *An actor is at most a poet and at least an entertainer.*

> *An actor's a guy who, if you ain't talking about him, ain't listening.*

> *The only thing an actor owes his public is not to bore them.*

> *Acting is like sustaining a twenty-five-year love affair. There are no new tricks. You just have to keep finding new ways to do it, to keep it fresh.*

He has a lot to say about typecasting and careerism:

> *If you play a pig, they think you're a pig.*

> *If you're successful, acting is about as soft a job as anybody could ever wish for. But if you're unsuccessful, it's worse than having a skin disease.*

> *Why should anybody care about what any movie star has to say? A movie star is nothing important. Freud, Gandhi, Marx—these people are important. But movie acting is just dull, boring, childish work. Movie stars are nothing as actors. I guess Garbo was the last one who had it.*

> *Quitting acting—that is the mark of maturity.*

He was once dubbed "Mumbles" for his characteristic way of talking:

> *In my own behavior with people, if I didn't trust or like someone, I would either say nothing or mumble. I got to be awfully good at mumbling.*

> *I suppose it's like the old Indian proverb about the leaf and the tree—"not a leaf moves that the tree does not know." Maybe a film does have an influence on people's lives.*

You could get the impression that he despises the profession that has made him famous:

> *I'm convinced that the larger the gross the worse the picture.*

> *The only reason I'm here is because I don't yet have the moral strength to turn down the money.*

> *After you've got enough money, money doesn't matter.*

And that he has a cynical view of human nature:

If we are not our brother's keeper, at least let us not be his executioner.

CLOSE-UPS

An angel as a man and a monster as an actor. — Bernardo Bertolucci

He constantly surprises me—he's the only one who does.
— Richard Burton

He's more than a man. He's an experience. — Bianca Jagger

He was antisocial because he knew society was crap; he was a hero to youth because he was strong enough not to take the crap.
— Pauline Kael

Don't believe Marlon. Don't tell me he searches inside himself for everything. He looks out, too. He's peripheral, just as any other character is peripheral. — Sir Laurence Olivier

Most of the time he sounds like he has a mouth full of wet toilet paper. — Rex Reed

CHARLES CHAPLIN

Although Charlie Chaplin (1889-1977) was knighted a few years before his death, the title Sir Charles sounds fabricated and inappropriate. Charlie is "a man of the people," a spokesman for "the little guy," not a titled Englishman. Such remains Chaplin's charm and calculation; he had the best of both worlds. Among his most popular full-length films are: *The Gold Rush* (1924), *City Lights* (1931), *Modern Times* (1936), *The Great Dictator* (1940), *Monsieur Verdoux* (1947), and *Limelight* (1952).

Here's a clue to Chaplin's immense popularity:

Frankly, I enjoy my comedies even more than the audience.

The secret of his comedy?

I had stumbled on the secret of being funny: an idea going in one direction meets an opposite idea suddenly.

Figuring out what the audience expects, and then doing something different, is great fun to me.

All I need to make a comedy is a park, a policeman, and a pretty girl.

Chaplin makes public his trade secrets:

You know this fellow is many-sided, a tramp, a gentleman, a poet, a dreamer, a lonely fellow, always hopeful of romance and adventure.

Don't be like the great majority of actors. . . don't just stand around waiting your turn to speak—learn to listen.

Once, at a reception, after claiming he couldn't sing a note, he sang a solo very successfully. He explained:

I can't sing at all—I was only imitating Caruso.

Other remarks about himself have a similar tone:

I am too tragic by nature to play Hamlet. Only a great comedian can act him.

What difference does it make whether I eat mustard with ice cream or put sugar in beer, except on the screen?

Whatever I do, I find myself wondering, "Now, will that be good for my work or not."

His philosophy of life?

I have no design for living, no philosophy—whether sage or fool, we must all struggle with life.

Perhaps the world's best known and loved person, he was lonely:

I was loved by crowds, but I didn't have a single close friend. . . I felt like the loneliest man alive.

Was he riddled with self-doubt? Perhaps, perhaps not:

You have to believe in yourself, that's the secret. Even when I was in the orphanage, when I was roaming the streets trying to find enough to eat to keep alive, even then I thought of myself as the greatest actor in the world. I had to feel the exuberance that comes from utter confidence in yourself. Without it you go down to defeat.

On his creation "Charlie," the "Little Man," and himself:

I am known in parts of the world by people who have never heard of Jesus Christ.

CLOSE-UPS

All I know about Mr. Chaplin, and all I ever want to know, is that, measuring my words and remembering all the great players, he is, in my view, the greatest of them all.— James Agate

To work with Chaplin, the greatest man in the movies! It meant that every ambition of mine as an actress would be fulfilled.— Claire Bloom

Charlie, Oona, and the two babies. They were like a tableau by Renoir.— Robert Florey

Charlie Chaplin is no businessman—all he knows is that he can't take anything less.— Sam Goldwyn

I know I should enjoy the California sunshine and meeting Charlie Chaplin.— H.G. Wells

Chaplin is the one man in the world I want to meet.— Nikolai Lenin

JOAN CRAWFORD

From flapper to tough-minded businesswoman, Joan Crawford (1906-1977) matured in the movies, played a multitude of roles, and personified the hopes and fears of millions of women the world over. She was every inch a pro, from her hard lips and sad eyes to her mannish style of dress. She appears to excellent advantage in *Grand Hotel* (1932), *The Women* (1939), *Mildred Pierce* (1945), *Sudden Fear* (1952), and *Whatever Happened to Baby Jane* (1962).

JOAN CRAWFORD 1928

Crawford could see clearly the complicity and ambiguity of the audience in her popularity:

> *The public likes provocative feminine personalities, but it also likes to know that, underneath it all, the actresses are ladies.*

Popular with reporters in the Forties and Fifties, she once said:

> *Why don't you say that you asked me about marriage, and I changed the subject.*

A characteristic remark of a professional:

> *If you think I made poor pictures after* A Woman's Face, *you should see the ones I went on suspension not to make!*

Crawford was, for many, the epitome of the working woman—the professional:

I like to work. Inactivity is one of the great indignities of life. Through inactivity, people lose their self-respect, their integrity. The need to work is always there, bugging me.

Actors and actresses, more than most of us, have their ups and downs. What is most important?

All I know is, I'm still here.

CLOSE-UPS

A star is when someone says, "Let's leave the dishes in the sink and go see Joan Crawford."— Clarence Brown

Joan Crawford is doubtless the best example of the flapper, the girl you see at smart night clubs, gowned to the apex of sophistication, toying iced glasses with a remote, faintly bitter expression, dancing deliciously, laughing a great deal, with wide, hurt eyes. Young things with a talent for living.— F. Scott Fitzgerald

Why can't Joan ever forget for a single second that she's Joan Crawford?— Alexander Kirkland

How splendid that Joan Crawford can still outstare us all!
— Michael Redgrave

One gal I really respect is Joan Crawford. Crawford the Indomitable. Whether she's on the set, or on the street, or plugging a picture, or plugging Pepsi-Cola, she's a star. That's her profession and she never lets you down.— Jerry Wald

The best time I ever had with Joan Crawford was when I pushed her down the stairs in Whatever Happened to Baby Jane.— Bette Davis

BETTE DAVIS

Dramatic is the word to describe Bette Davis, born in 1908, and independent is another. Unlike Tallulah Bankhead, Davis found excellent roles in movies, for her films include *Of Human Bondage* (1934), *The Petrified Forest* (1936), *All About Eve* (1950), in which she played Margo Channing, and *Whatever Happened to Baby Jane* (1962), where she played opposite Joan Crawford. She entitled her 1962 autobiography *The Lonely Life.*

She has an impulsive—and friendly—manner:

Call me Bette or we'll never be friends.

And no illusions about inspiration:

When they see me on the screen, they're seeing thirty-seven years of sweat.

Her advice to a young actress?

What would I tell a young actress starting out today? Take care of

BETTE
DAVIS
1943

your health. Deny yourself fun like you'll never know. And when you make a picture, you have to say, "This is all I do." Pretty bloody boring, if you think about it.

Of her craft she said:

The real actor—like any real artist—has a direct line to the collective heart.

I learn the lines and pray to God.

And about Hollywood?

We had the answer, the successor, or the sequel to everything.

On her checkered marital life:

Would I consider remarriage? If I found a man who had $15,000,000, would sign over half of it to me before the marriage, and guarantee he'd be dead within a year.

Bette's a woman with drive:

I am determined to die with my name above the titles.

The reason for her success?

I survived because I was tougher than everybody else.

Once Bette Davis trusts you, she's marvellous. — Robert Aldrich

She deserves. . . the admiration of countless millions of movie fans for making women on the screen the fascinating creatures they are in real life. — Alex Barris

Bette Davis has as much sex appeal as Slim Summerville.
— Carl Laemmle

Whatever Bette would have chosen to do in life, she would have had to be the top or she couldn't have endured it. — ex-husband, Gary Merrill

The saying around Hollywood:

Nobody's as good as Bette when she's bad.

MARLENE DIETRICH

Marlene Dietrich, never a great actress, but always an intriguing one, was born in Germany in 1901. Is there a touch of sado-masochism in her manner? Her films include: *The Blue Angel* (1930), *Shanghai Express* (1932), *Destry Rides Again* (1939), *Witness for the Prosecution* (1957), *Touch of Evil* (1958), and *Judgment at Nuremberg* (1961). She may not know the meaning of the word glamor, but perhaps, that's only because she herself defines the word.

Marlene Dietrich, who drives others to superlatives, talks about herself in diminutives:

I have a child. And I have made a few people happy. That is all. . . .

She separates her personal from her public life with a wall of words:

It is my private life which no one knows anything about, nor ever will. It needs more than half my time if it is to be a success.

Of her mannish style of dress she says:

I dress for the image, not for myself, not for the public, not for fashion, not for men.

She's:

. . . tired of being called a sexy grandmother. Arthur Rubinstein is a great artist, but who gives a damn how many grandchildren he has?

She alludes to her uniqueness:

There is probably some country where they say, "Dietrich—who the hell is she?" Well, I wouldn't go there.

About marriage, sex and happiness:

To make a man happy is a full-time job—with no holidays.

The average man is more interested in a woman who is interested in him than he is in a woman with beautiful legs.

A man would prefer to come home to an unmade bed and a happy woman than to a neatly made bed and an angry woman.

Tenderness is greater proof of love than the most passionate of vows.

On sex generally:

In America an obsession. In other parts of the world, a fact.

One thing counts:

Quality: There is nothing better.

One thing she can't define:

Glamor: The which I would like to know the meaning of.

On friends:

It's the ones you can call up at 4:00 a.m. who matter.

All my friends are dead.

She sees her career and its inevitable end this way:

Of course I'm going to quit working. I want a chance to really see a bit of life before I die.

A film star's career must necessarily be brief. It can last only as long as one's youth lasts, and one's youth fades far quicker on the screen than on the stage. The public can be fooled on the stage, but never on the screen—and I'm going to quit while I'm still at the top.

Right now the thing that worries me most is that if I do not get back to the theater, there will be no opening night.

Dietrich has one "enormous preference":

When I die, I'd like to be buried in Paris. But I'd also like to leave my heart in England. And in Germany—nothing.

CLOSE-UPS

Marlene Dietrich? I adore her—the most beautiful woman I've ever met. In a curious way like a skeleton risen from the grave, face-bones barely covered with make-up. Arise, oh beautiful bones. Beautiful and extraordinary. Besides, she cooks well.— Richard Burton

You are (all sails flying) a frigate, a figurehead, a Chinese fish, a lyrebird, a legend, and a wonder.—Jean Cocteau

I know that every time I've seen Marlene Dietrich, it has done something to my heart.— Ernest Hemingway

Marlene Dietrich is not an actress, like Sarah Bernhardt: she is a myth, like Phryne.— André Malraux

Dietrich—well, she will always be Dietrich. Fastidious to a degree and a genius at spending your money.— Stanley Kramer

CLARK GABLE

Clark Gable (1901-1960) was a man's man. It's hard to explain exactly what is meant by that, but every man—and woman—who saw him on the screen caught the masculine message. Gable was not outstanding as an actor, but he worked hard and left his manly mark on many films, including: *Red Dust* (1932), *It Happened One Night* (1934), *San Francisco* (1936), *Gone With the Wind* (1939), as Rhett Butler, *The Hucksters* (1947), and *The Misfits* (1960). Clark Gable was known as "The King"—presumably of Hollywood:

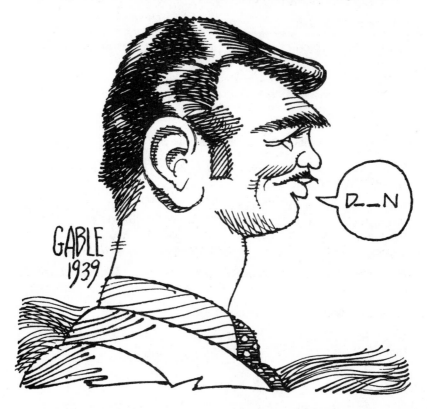

You know, this King stuff is pure bullshit. I eat and sleep and go to the bathroom just like everyone else. There's no special light that shines and makes me a star. I'm just a lucky slob from Ohio. I happened to be in the right place at the right time, and I had a lot of smart guys helping me—that's all.

Stardom didn't seem to delude him:

The only thing that kept me a big star has been revivals of *Gone With the Wind*. Every time that picture is re-released, a whole new crop of young moviegoers gets interested in me.

He sounds basically pragmatic about the whole thing:

I want the most because you're only important if you get it.

> *It's hard enough for me to act without going into all those monkey-shines. What I want to do is get the money. Let others get the grief.*

Gable came up on the screen as a real person:

> *Talent is the least important thing a performer needs, but humility is one thing he must have.*

Once, at a dinner party, he asked:

> *Do you write, Mr. Faulkner?*

And on sex:

> *It's an extra dividend when you like the girl you're in love with.*

A final request to his wife:

> *If anything ever happens to me, don't let them make a circus out of it.*

CLOSE-UPS

> *His ears are too big. He looks like an ape.*— Darryl F. Zanuck

> *Clark Gable was the King of an empire called Hollywood. The empire is not what it once was—but the King has not been dethroned, even after death.*— Joan Crawford

> *You know how much I love Pappy, but to tell you the honest truth, he isn't such a hell of a good lay.*— Carole Lombard

> *Clark Gable has the best ears of our lives.*— Milton Berle

> *Oh, Gable has enemies, all right—but they all like him.*
> — David O. Selznick

> *On the screen...Gable...absolutely comes over as he is.*
> — Rex Harrison

GRETA GARBO

No one will ever know the secrets of the Sphinx, or those of Greta Garbo, who was born in Sweden in 1905. Even after forty years of retirement, she remains an enigma. Among her best pictures are *Anna Christie* (1930), *Mata Hari* (1931), *Grand Hotel* (1932), *Queen Christina* (1933), *Camille* (1936), and *Ninotchka* (1939). Subsequent offers to play Sarah Bernhardt and George Sand she declined—to our loss.

Greta Garbo took pains with reporters, when she was still speaking to them, to explain that she did not say, "I want to be alone."

> *I never said "I want to be alone." I only said, "I want to be let alone." There is all the difference.*

The line itself comes from *Grand Hotel* (1932). She went on to say:

> *I've become afraid of life. . . .*

GARBO
1939

> *I love no one.*

On other occasions:

> *Well, gentlemen. As usual I have nothing to say!*
>
> *I give them everything I've got on the screen—why do they try to usurp my privacy?*
>
> *The truth is, I feel able to express myself only through my roles, not in words, and that is why I try to avoid talking to the press.*

Is there something fatalistic here? At the height of her fame, she explained:

> *I knew I was too happy.*
>
> *How wonderful to be happy for no reason.*

And then later:

> *Dead? Dead? I have been dead many years.*
>
> *I said no so many times, and now it's too late.*

CLOSE-UPS

Garbo to me is a never-ending source of wonder. — Clarence Brown

By being worshipped by the entire world, she gives you the feeling that, if your imagination has to sin, it can at least congratulate itself on its impeccable taste. — Alistair Cooke

One almost feels grateful to Garbo for keeping herself so resolutely to herself, for leaving us a little mystery. — Joan Crawford

She has a magic quality which will survive bad pictures—and even age. . . . — Marlene Dietrich

Garbo. No. Garbo! Better. — Garson Kanin

I would rather spend an hour with Greta than a lifetime with any other woman. — John Gilbert

In the full flower of their romance, Gilbert and Garbo were added by movie fans to the list of immortal lovers: Romeo and Juliet, Dante and Beatrice, Antony and Cleopatra. — Adele Rogers St. Johns

Gary Cooper and Greta Garbo are the same person. After all, have you ever seen them in a movie together? — Ernst Lubitsch

Garbo, Greta—a deer, in the body of a woman, living resentfully in the Hollywood zoo. — Clare Boothe Luce

Tell her that, in America, men don't like fat women. — Louis B. Mayer

Making a film with Greta Garbo does not constitute an introduction.
— Robert Montgomery

After much brooding and reappraisal, I still cannot make up my mind whether Garbo was a remarkable actress or simply a person so extraordinary that she made everything she did, even acting, seem remarkable. — Isabel Quigley

Garbo was the only one we could kill off. The Shearer and Crawford pictures had to end with a clinch, but the women seemed to enjoy watching Garbo die. — J. Robert Rubin

Her name is Greta Garbo. She will be one of our greatest actresses.
— Mauritz Stiller

Garbo's peculiar art has always been to say, in essence, to the male audience: "Don't forget that I am only an image, and that is all I can be to you." — Parker Tyler

What, when drunk, one sees in other women, one sees in Garbo sober. — Kenneth Tynan

JUDY GARLAND

Judy Garland (1922-69) began her career as a child star and remained something of the little girl all her life. She acted and sang with a nervous gusto; in the end, she wore herself out and died exhausted. Not without reason was she called the American Edith Piaf. She performed notably in *The Wizard of Oz* (1939), *For Me and My Gal* (1942), *Meet Me in St. Louis* (1944), *Easter Parade* (1948), *A Star is Born* (1954), and *Judgment at Nuremberg* (1961).

Judy Garland was literally "born in a trunk."

> *I was born at the age of twelve on the Metro-Goldwyn-Mayer lot.*

She expressed optimism about life, even when down:

> *All you have to do is never cheat and work your best and work your hardest, and they'll respond to you.*

> *The only time I felt accepted or wanted was when I was on stage.*

Ups and downs:

> *It's lonely and cold on top.*

> *What comeback? I've never been away.*

> *What do I do when I'm down? I put on my lipstick, see my stockings are straight, and go out there and sing "Over the Rainbow."*

About that song?

> *I've got rainbows up my ass, honey!*

CLOSE-UPS

> *Judy didn't die of anything, except wearing out. She just plain wore out.* — Ray Bolger

> *I don't think you've read the finish of Judy Garland yet. She'll come back. She's unpredictable—this girl will come back.*
> *"Over the Rainbow" was taken out of the film after a preview, but I had it put back in before the picture was released.* — Arthur Freed

> *I don't care how long I wait for that girl—I'd wait forever for that Garland magic.* — Van Johnson

> *I've never in my life seen an audience pull for a singer the way they pull for Judy Garland.*
> *She's beautiful, an angel—with spurs.* — Joe Pasternak

> *Watching Judy Garland, I have a surge of affection...it is for something beyond acting that one cherishes this vivid, elated little creature...it is for the true star's quality. The quality of being.*
> — Dilys Powell

> *Mother was the real-life Wicked Witch of the West.* — Liza Minnelli

CARY GRANT

Cary Grant, born in England in 1904, played in pictures for forty years before he received an Oscar, awarded in 1970 for no special role but simply for "sheer brilliance." His specialty? The man-about-town, whose touch is light and comic. Among his many films are: *She Done Him Wrong* (1933), *Topper* (1937), *Bringing Up Baby* (1938), *The Philadelphia Story* (1940), *Mr. Blandings Builds His Dream House* (1948), and *North by Northwest* (1959).

Cary Grant is a reporter's delight:

> *I improve on misquotation.*

He's forever making light of his life and work:

> *I get up in the morning, go to bed at night, and occupy myself as best I can in between.*

> *It's really a great comedy, this business of living. Why can't movie writers write about it that way?*

Yet beneath the debonaire manner:

> *I often think my life has been a failure. But whenever I drop into a theater and hear women laughing at one of my films, I think, well, if I brightened their day before they went home and did the dishes, maybe my life wasn't wasted after all.*

Is he type-cast. . .as himself?

> *The character I play best is me, Cary Grant.*

> *Why interfere with success?*

Marriage has never been one of his strong points:

> *Having children gives a man confidence. A man should fill up a woman with children.*

> *All my wives were my favorites.*

> *Twin beds disunite you. All this His and Hers is a lot of rot.*

> *When I am married, I want to be single, and when I am single, I want to be married.*

The note of realism that crept into theater and film in the 1960's was not to his liking:

> *Is a garbage can any more real than Buckingham Palace?*

Making movies is great:

> *Do you know of any other business where a man can earn a million dollars in ten weeks?*

Has he retired?

> Why haven't I made a film since 1966? It was time to climb off the celluloid and join the real world.

On longevity:

> I'm reminded of what someone said: "If I had known I was going to live this long, I'd have taken better care of myself."

An editor sent the handsome star.the following telegram:

> How old Cary Grant?

The star replied:

> Old Cary Grant fine. How you?

CLOSE-UPS

> I loved sinking my head into Cary Grant's chest.— Jean Arthur

> I learned courage from Buddha, Jesus, Lincoln, Einstein, and Cary Grant.— Peggy Lee

KATHARINE HEPBURN & SPENCER TRACY

What a quarrelsome, loving couple: Katharine Hepburn, classy, spirited; Tracy, rugged, plodding. They were good separately; together they were even better. Together they made: Woman of the Year (1942), Keeper of the Flame (1942), State of the Union (1948), Adam's Rib (1949), Pat and Mike (1952), The Desk Set (1957), and Guess Who's Coming to Dinner (1967).

Hepburn, born in 1909, appeared to great effect in Bringing Up Baby (1938), The Philadelphia Story (1940), The African Queen (1951), Long Day's Journey into Night (1962), and A Delicate Balance (1973). Her image off screen and on is one of marvellous openness and common sense.

Tracy (1900-67), who made his stage debut as a robot in R.U.R. in 1922, appeared in such films as Fury (1936), Boys' Town (1938), Father of the Bride (1950), Bad Day at Black Rock (1955), The Last Hurrah (1958), Inherit the Wind (1960), and Judgment at Nuremberg (1961).

Here's Hepburn on life in general, and acting in particular.

> Life's what's important. Walking, houses, family. Birth and pain and joy—and then death. Acting's just waiting for a custard pie. That's all.

Youth is fine. . .for the young:

> The idea that everyone wants to keep his body eternally seventeen is bloody wrong nonsense.

KATHARINE
HEPBURN
1937

On being a star:

> I'm a personality as well as an actress. Show me an actress who isn't a personality, and you'll show me a woman who isn't a star. A star's personality has to shine through.

> I only want to go on being a star. It's all I know how to be.

Does she look back in sorrow?

> I don't regret anything I've ever done—so long as I enjoyed doing it at the time.

There is a secret to acting:

> If you give audiences a chance, they'll do half your acting for you.

On interviews:

> I don't care what is written about me—so long as it isn't true.

When it came to her co-star, she could never be more generous:

> Everyone loves Mr. Tracy.

CLOSE-UPS

Ever since I got into this business, people have been trying to interview me for magazines because I'm Katharine Hepburn's niece, so I've developed a format letter I've sent around saying, "If you promise that you will not mention Katharine Hepburn, I would be happy to give you an interview."— Katharine Houghton

I like Katharine Hepburn in anything.— F. Scott Fitzgerald

Katharine Hepburn runs the gamut of emotions from A to B.
— Dorothy Parker

Tracy had Katharine Hepburn down pat:

The trouble with Kate is she understands me.

When a director complained that Hepburn was too tall for him:

Don't worry, Miss Hepburn, I'll soon cut you down to my size.

On accepting an Oscar for *Boys' Town*:

If you have seen Father Flanagan through me, then I thank you.

Tracy on acting:

Acting is not an important job in the scheme of things. Plumbing is.

I'm getting old, and I've never done a picture with Capra.

Well, it's taken me forty years of doing it for a living to learn the secret. I don't know that I want to give it away. Okay, I'll tell you. The secret of acting is—learn your lines!

A plain man, you might say:

Look, I'm too old, too tired and too goddam rich for all this bull. Let's just get on with the scene.

CLOSE-UPS

All he has to do is show up and be photographed.— Clark Gable

In my adult years, the man I have admired most in acting is Spencer Tracy. What an actor should be is exemplified, for me, by him.
— Richard Widmark

SIR LAURENCE OLIVIER

Sir Laurence, now Lord Olivier, is the screen Shakespearian *par excellence*, and virtually without equal as a light comedian and character actor. He was born in England in 1907, is a former director of National Theatre in London, and has been a West End and Broadway favorite for decades. Among his greatest films are *Wuthering Heights* (1939), *Pride and Prejudice* (1940), *Henry V* (1944), *Hamlet* (1948), *Richard III* (1954), *The Entertainer* (1960), and *Othello* (1966). He has appeared in many more-recent films, giving great character to essentially ephemeral roles.

Sir Laurence is not taken with esoteric theories of acting:

> *You need to be a bit of a bastard to be a star.*

> *Acting is just one big bag of tricks.*

Nor does he worry about "relating" to the audience:

> *What is the main problem of the actor? It is to keep the audience awake and not let them go to sleep, then wake up and go home feeling they've wasted their money.*

He has mastered light comic characterizations:

> *A comedian is closer to humanity than a tragedian. He learns not to take himself seriously.*

He once lectured theater students on the different kinds of truth:

> *The difference between the actual truth and the illusion of truth is what you are about to learn. You will not finish learning it until you are dead.*

Criticized for declaiming rather than reciting Shakespeare's lines, he admitted:

> *I think I'm associated more with trumpets than with strings.*

CLOSE-UPS

Olivier is a comedian by instinct and a tragedian by art. — James Agate

I believe Laurence Olivier to be the greatest actor of our time.
> — Sir Noël Coward

Laurence Olivier is never dull. The voice, however, has more the quality of brass than of strings. — Sir Tyrone Guthrie

Ironically enough, Laurence Olivier is less gifted than Marlon Brando. He is even less gifted than Richard Burton, Paul Scofield, Ralph Richardson and John Gielgud. But he is still the definitive actor of the Twentieth Century. — William Redfield

There is something animal-like about him—like the King of the Jungle. . . . — Joan Plowright

I see Sir Laurence as a rhinoceros. — Salvador Dali

MARY PICKFORD & DOUGLAS FAIRBANKS

Their names are united in Pickfair, their Hollywood mansion, for so many years the center around which the film community in Hollywood turned. Mary and Doug were married in 1920 and, until their divorce in 1935, were—next to the King and Queen of England—the world's best-known couple.

Mary Pickford (1893-1979), though born in Canada, established herself in silent films as "America's Sweetheart," a little girl with long golden curls, appearing in such films as *Rebecca of Sunnybrook Farm* (1917), *Pollyanna* (1919), and *Little Annie Rooney* (1925).

Douglas Fairbanks (1883-1939), the ever-smiling hero of swashbuckling costume adventures dashed through such pictures as: *The Mark of Zorro* (1920), *The Three Musketeers* (1921), *Robin Hood* (1921), *The Thief of Baghdad* (1923), and *The Private Life of Don Juan* (1934).

The two appeared opposite each other in their first talking picture, *The Taming of the Shrew* (1929). She never did sell Pickfair but lived there in seclusion with her husband Buddy Rogers. Doug's son by an earlier marriage, Douglas Fairbanks, Jr., born in 1909, has appeared in such action films as *The Prisoner of Zenda* (1937) and *Sinbad the Sailor* (1947).

Pickford was clear-eyed about her appeal:

> *I didn't ask to be anybody's idol. I'm merely an actress playing children on the screen.*

She never felt completely natural on the set:

> *I don't remember ever stepping before a camera without a certain dread.*

She had a firm sense of her image:

> *A prominent Hollywood producer asked me if I would relinquish the title of "America's Sweetheart" for a promising young protégée of his. I answered that the title wasn't mine to give, that, in fact, I had never accepted it, but that, such as it was, it had been conferred upon me as a gesture of love by an old and beloved friend.*

Her career didn't altogether please her:

> *I'm not exactly satisfied, but I'm grateful, and that's a very different thing.*

> *I would rather be a beautiful memory in the minds of people, than a horrible example on celluloid.*

When she cut off her golden tresses, she became another woman—in the eyes of her public:

> *I sometimes wonder whether I had the right to cut off my hair. Were the choice ever given to me again, I am positive I would not do it.*

> *I made up my mind to step into the wings while the audience was still applauding.*

CLOSE-UPS

Well, my little friend, from now on your name will be Mary Pickford, and will you come back, please, with your aunt, tomorrow night and see our play?— David Belasco

Mary Pickford had everything Chaplin had, and was much prettier too.— Eileen Bowser

There was something heavenly about Mary Pickford!— James Card

Say anything you like but don't say I like to work. That sounds too much like Mary Pickford, that prissy bitch.— Mabel Normand

She's been sick, you know. She was "My Best Girl" in 1927 and she's still my best girl.— Buddy Rogers

Fairbanks, for a romantic hero, sounds remarkably unromantic in his outlook:

The best movie actors are children and animals.

He was aware he cut a distinctive swath through the world:

Aw, but nobody can take my place.

To Mary Pickford, with the advent of sound:

Aw, Mary, nobody cares anything about us any more, let's sell Pickfair and move to Switzerland and just get old.

On a well-timed retirement:

When a man finds himself sliding downhill, he should do everything to reach bottom in a hurry and pass out of the picture.

CLOSE-UPS

My father's footsteps were so light that they left no trace for anyone to follow. My respect for his work is so considerable that I don't believe anyone could successfully emulate them.

I don't think that married people ought to be conscious of the fact that they are married. They ought to live in sin, so to speak.
— Douglas Fairbanks, Jr.

Douglas Fairbanks' death has robbed the movies of a bit of themselves—a drop of the lifeblood that first made them gay, great, and indomitable.— C.A. Lejeune

ELIZABETH TAYLOR

Elizabeth Taylor, born in England in 1932, has managed to cram into a relatively short span of years a lot of living, loving, and film-making. She started out as a child star with movies like *Lassie Come Home* (1943) and *National Velvet* (1944), grew up to play in *A Place in the Sun* (1951) and *Giant* (1956), moved into maturity with *Cat on a Hot Tin Roof* (1958), and matched a silly performance in *Cleopatra* (1962) with a serious one in *Who's Afraid of Virginia Woolf?* (1966). Her marital life commands even more attention than her films.

Taylor is not at all maudlin in her self-appraisals:

> *I have the face and body of a woman and the mind of a child.*

> *My toughest role was learning to grow up.*

> *If someone was stupid enough to offer me a million dollars to make a picture—I was certainly not dumb enough to turn it down.*

She responds to biting criticism:

> *When people say, "She's got everything," I've only one answer: "I haven't had tomorrow."*

Love and marriage do not always go together:

> *Marriage is like a very good recipe. After you've made it and put in every ingredient, you can't let it sit in the icebox too long. You have to stir it occasionally, and add a touch of this or that flavor.*

> *What do you expect me to do? Sleep alone?*

> *Unless something comes along that absolutely captivates me, the "life of leisure" is for me—if you call being married to Richard Burton and the mother of four leisure.*

On being cast as the lead in *Cleopatra*:

> *It will be fun to be the first Jewish Queen of Egypt.*

Schoolgirls yearn for stardom; stars yearn to be ordinary:

> *Beauty? Who wants it? I want a home in a quiet place, where no one knows my name, except the grocer, the butcher, and the milkman.*

A wry twist:

> *I'm Mother Courage. I'll be dragging my sable coat behind me into old age.*

> *The price of food is going up, and diamonds, too.*

> *I think I've licked life at every level.*

Her own epitaph:

> HERE LIES ELIZABETH TAYLOR
> THANK YOU FOR EVERY MOMENT, GOOD AND BAD
> I'VE ENJOYED IT ALL!

CLOSE-UPS

Sympathy would be on my side if the people knew the whole story of our marriage.— Eddie Fisher

Miss Taylor and her husband must have discovered by now what the Bible could have told them long ago, that there is, unfortunately, no way to invent a new sin.— Richard Griffith

Elizabeth Taylor knows more about suffering than Charles Dickens and St. Augustine put together.— Laurence Harvey

It must be sad to be an Elizabeth Taylor, who hasn't been to a supermarket for ten years.— Joanne Woodward

JOHN WAYNE

His weather-beaten features are those of a survivor, a veteran's veteran. Wayne, (1907-1979), a former football player, has appeared in innumerable action films, notably: *The Big Trail* (1930), *Red River* (1948), *She Wore a Yellow Ribbon* (1949), *Sands of Iwo Jima* (1949), *Rio Bravo* (1959), *The Alamo* (1960), *The Green Berets* (1968), and *True Grit* (1969). He had Screen Presence. He is Mr. America personified.

Wayne was wise in his own way, and painstakingly precise about himself:

> *Sometimes I wonder about my career. I don't do much really, I suppose. Just sell sincerity. And I've been selling the hell out of it ever since I got going.*

He had a precise view of himself as a screen actor:

> *In fact, I don't even call myself an actor. I'm a reactor. I listen to what the other guy is saying, and I react to it. That's the John Wayne method.*

> *John Ford taught me what to do in front of the movie camera. He taught me not to act but to react.*

He understood the role of that "something extra" an actor must possess:

> *You get lost on the screen if your personality doesn't show through.*

It is hard not to see the man's man here:

> *I would like to be remembered—well, the Mexicans have an expression, feo, fuerte y formal, which means: He was ugly, was strong, and had dignity.*

Wayne frequently replied to criticism of his "my country right or wrong" attitude:

> *It's kind of a sad thing when a normal love of country makes you a superpatriot.*

Retirement and death are not lightly regarded:

> *They can stop hiring this old horse and put him out to pasture—but I'll never go of my own accord.*

> *I licked the Big C with love of God and a lot of guts.*

CLOSE-UP

John Wayne has an endless face and he can go on forever.
> — Louis B. Mayer

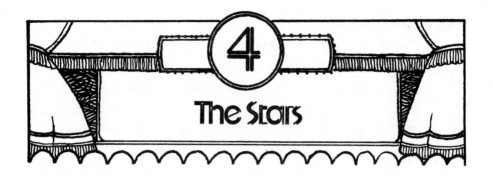

4

The Stars

If one takes seriously the interviews with film stars that appear regularly in newspapers and magazines, it would appear that actors and actresses are not busy people at all, but have great stretches of time with nothing to do but sit around with reporters and interviewers, talk about themselves, reminisce about their careers, and spell out their hopes and fears. Indeed, the convention of the interview—media exposure situation—requires garrulousness on the part of the interviewee and calculated impersonality on the interviewer's part, many of whom have heard it all before and know better.

Yet, on occasion, something is said that is worth preserving—a notion, a phrase, an insight, an image, an expression so characteristic of the speaker that it strikes resonant chords in everyone who has ever seen that actor or actress on the stage or screen. Sometimes, too, the remark reveals an unsuspected facet of a favorite peronality's character. Thus we find out a new fact about an old friend, or about ourselves. Sometimes a remark is just so funny or so wise, so outrageous or so clever, so touching or just plain beautiful, that we shouldn't let it get lost.

Each of us has film footage buried within ourselves. A name or a face will start up the projector in the psyche. As the artist Harold Town mused:

> I'd like to make a science-fiction cosmic distillator that could synthesize all the random bits of one actor's ambience hidden in yesterday's fans and project the monumental image on the blue sky on a clear summer day!

EDDIE ALBERT:
No one but an actor can run the gamut of life's experiences.

JUNE ALLYSON:
I always wanted to be a movie star. I thought it meant being famous and having breakfast in bed. I didn't know you had to be up at 4:00 a.m.

DAME JUDITH ANDERSON:
Having been made a Dame [by the Queen] has made a slight difference in my life. I find myself wearing gloves more often.

DANA ANDREWS:
I believe that all people are half actors.

47

JULIE ANDREWS:

How does it feel to be a star? I suck my thumb a lot.

ANNE-MARGRET:

I am delighted to be back—I am delighted to be anywhere.

A man who is honest with himself wants a woman to be soft and feminine, careful of what she's saying, and to talk like a man.

EVE ARDEN:

I've worked with a lot of great glamorous girls in movies and the theater. And I'll admit, I've often thought it would be wonderful to be a femme fatale. But then I'd always come back to thinking that if they only had what I've had—a family, real love, an anchor—they would have been so much happier during all the hours when the marquees and the footlights are dark.

ARLETTY, French tragedienne:

If you have enemies, it is because in some way you want them, and that is terrible.

JEAN ARTHUR:

The fact that I did not marry George Bernard Shaw is the only real disappointment I've had.

MARY ASTOR:

I was neither a peacock nor the girl next door, and heads turning in my direction always gave me sweaty palms.

You can't make anything be Art—and the minute you try, it eludes you. And if you behave like an artist, you'll never be one.

We were the hope peddlers; we pushed it in all sorts of brightly colored capsules: Love Conquers All, Crime Doesn't Pay, Honesty Is the Best Policy, Hard Work Reaps Rewards, The Rich Are Unhappy—the Poor Are Happy, Good Triumphs Over Evil. These silver linings to all clouds were the stuff of dreams, and human beings like to dream.

RICHARD ATTENBOROUGH:

It's my honest belief. . . that it's much more edifying and aesthetically pleasing to have a beautiful painting to look at than a healthy bank balance.

CHARLES AZNAVOUR, on happiness and success:

What can you tell about happiness? But about sadness there is much to say. It is real and more interesting than gaiety.

Success is the result of a collective hallucination simulated by the artist.

JIM BACKUS:

Many a man owes his success to his first wife—and his second wife to his success.

BARBARA BAIN:

Too many girls think about what they are going to receive rather than what they are going to give....It's a case that when love flows thick, faults flow thin.

CARROLL BAKER:

In the end, it led to a kind of nervous breakdown. When I came out of it, I realized I was faced with two choices: the way out that Marilyn Monroe took, or to run away. I just ran.

LUCILLE BALL:

The days in my life that stand out most vividly are the days I've learned something.

I have to work or I am nothing.

I just try to be good.

ANNE BANCROFT:

I'm going back to New York, where an over-sized bosom doesn't take priority over reading your lines.

LEX BARKER:

If you're an actor, it's always hard to be married.

ANNE BAXTER:

I'm an actress first and last. I don't want any of this whole shmeer about being a movie star.

See into life; don't just look at it.

Best to have failure happen early. It wakes up the phoenix bird in you.

WARREN BEATTY:

Marriage is a lie. How can you stand up and vow you'll stay together for life, when all the time you know you'll stick it out only while it's good?

WALLACE BEERY:

Like my dear old friend, Marie Dressler, my mug has been my fortune.

HARRY BELAFONTE:

I was standing in front of the bathroom mirror, brushing my teeth, and suddenly it hit me: "It's my teeth," I thought. "It's my goddam teeth!" Every time I open my mouth, every time I smile, my whole face lights up!

JEAN-PAUL BELMONDO:

Women over thirty are at their best, but men over thirty are too old to recognize it.

ROBERT BENCHLEY:

I am the oldest living man—especially at seven in the morning.

I must step out of these wet things and into a dry martini.

I'm glad this question came up, in a way, because there are so many different ways to answer it that one of them is bound to be right.

CONSTANCE BENNETT:

No! Five years from now, when I am married and have a family, I don't want pictures of me in underwear staring at me from the Police Gazette.

If you think I'm bad, you should see Claudette Colbert. Mind you, that's why she's Claudette Colbert.

CANDICE BERGEN:

I always thought "actress" was synonymous with "fool."

Most men are such jerks about beautiful women, it's hard not to despise them.

The best thing that's happened to the movie industry is its collapse.

INGRID BERGMAN:

In America people think, if they buy their tickets, they own you.

Happiness is good health—and a bad memory.

To survive in this business, you need a short memory and the constitution of an ox.

What you bring to an art is what you have within you. It's your very first intuition about a part that comes out in the end.

Tomorrow again today?

MILTON BERLE:

Life is very simple. The first thing to remember about life is—don't worry about it.

JACQUELINE BISSET:

Marriage seems to be a word which finishes a relationship. It doesn't start it. I think people should stop talking about people living together and start living themselves.

HONOR BLACKMAN:

The British just can't believe that a woman over thirty-five can be sexy.

CLAIRE BLOOM:
The problem of fading beauty in a woman is one of the powerful themes not only of drama, but of life itself.

DIRK BOGARDE:
I am the male Claudette Colbert. In all of sixty films, they always only shot my left.

According to American critics, I don't make "great" movies. I make "art" films in which I'm great.

Do I really need all this at the age of fifty-three?

SHIRLEY BOOTH:
Acting is a way to overcome your own inhibitions and shyness. The writer creates a strong, confident personality, and that's what you become—unfortunately, only for the moment.

ERNEST BORGNINE:
Acting is a matter of calculated instinct.

CHARLES BOYER:
I can say "wiz the" or I can say "with ze." But "with the" is impossible!

ROSSANO BRAZZI:
Sometimes my face is more beautiful than the leading lady's.

WALTER BRENNAN, on why he played so many different roles:
I'd rather do anything than sit around and wait for the undertaker.

FANNY BRICE:
Men always fall for frigid women because they put on the best show.

Thirty years of show business, and I had a hit as a four-year-old baby. I guess that's what you call the magic of radio!

CHARLES BRONSON:
I'm not one of my favorite actors.

LOUISE BROOKS:
The great art of films does not consist of descriptive movements of face and body, but in the movements of thought and soul transmitted in a kind of intense isolation.

VANESSA BROWN:
In Hollywood having a mind is all right—if you conceal it behind a low-cut bosom.

YUL BRUNNER:
Girls have an unfair advantage over men. If they can't get what they want by being smart, they can get it by being dumb.

Just call me a nice, clean-cut Mongolian boy.

GENEVIÈVE BUJOLD:
We're on the journey alone. Today is today, and yesterday I don't want to remember, and tomorrow I don't want to know about.

As soon as they say "Action," I can smell in the first two seconds whether I am going to get on the wave or not. And if you don't get on, you have this disastrous feeling. I can tell you—it's like love without climax.

BILLIE BURKE, early in her career:
I am neatly typed today, of course, possibly irrevocably typed, although I sincerely hope not, for I should like better parts.

CAROLE BURNETT:
Doing a movie is like being pregnant: you've got that terrible long wait to see if it's ugly.

RICHARD BURTON:
We Welsh are a strange people. That's how the word "welshing" came into being.

Unless you love someone, nothing makes any sense.

SID CAESAR:
The trouble with telling a good story is that it invariably reminds the other fellow of a dull one.

JAMES CAGNEY, on the secret of effective acting:
Walk in; plant yourself; look the other fellow in the eye, and tell the truth.

It doesn't make any difference how competent an actor you may be, if the public doesn't want to see you any more, you're all washed up.

MICHAEL CAINE:
When you start out broke and a nobody, what can anybody ever do to you?

You know, the thing that surprises people about me is that they expect to meet Alfie—and when they talk to me, they find a gardener.

MRS. PATRICK CAMPBELL, British leading lady, on breaking into the movies:
I'm over at Metro-Goldwyn-Mayer. I'm one of Norma Shearer's Nubian slaves.

Experience? Edward the Seventh.

DYAN CANNON:
My life as a woman is more important than my life as an actress.

EDDIE CANTOR:
The two most common causes of divorce? Men and women.

CLAUDIA CARDINALE:
To know women deeply, you have to like them or love them. Our movie profession is filled with men who don't like women.

KITTY CARLISLE:
TV cameras seem to add ten pounds to me. So I make it a policy never to eat TV cameras.

LESLIE CARON:
I don't think Hollywood is an appropriate place for an actress of forty.

DIAHANN CARROLL, on her domestic arrangements:
We don't believe in engagements—we believe in happiness.

LEO G. CARROLL:
As an actor, I don't mind being talked about—you have to be, if you want to stay in the business. It's just that I don't like being talked to.

MADELEINE CARROLL:
Producers don't look at you as a man looks at a woman; they look at you as if they were judging a horse.

JACK CARSON:
A fan club is a group of people who tell an actor he's not alone in the way he feels about himself.

JACK CARTER, to another actor:
You have a wonderful style. Unfortunately, it's mine.

JOAN CAULFIELD, on the Hollywood of the Forties:
I miss the glamor, the beauty, the gaiety—the mystique that movie people had in those days.

RICHARD CHAMBERLAIN:
I suddenly had a hunch that the things I really wanted to know—like how to speak, act, move and feel—could only be found in England. So I went there to see if they would let me in.

CAROL CHANNING:
Laughter is much more important than applause. Applause is almost a duty. Laughter is a reward. Laughter means they trust and like you.

GERALDINE CHAPLIN:
If you want to start a career, any career, and your name is Chaplin, you don't have the slightest difficulty getting started.

MAURICE CHEVALIER:
> An artist carries on, throughout his life, a mysterious, uninterrupted conversation with his public.

PETULA CLARK:
> I thank God to be out of the country when my old movies come back on late-night television.

SUSAN CLARK, on her burgeoning career:
> I've travelled, met fascinating movie people, and generally had a hell of a good time. No regrets, Mr. True Confessions.

MONTGOMERY CLIFT:
> I am neither a young rebel, nor an old rebel, nor a tired rebel but, quite simply, an actor who tries to do his job with the maximum of conviction and certainty.

> An actor must share experiences familiar to the audience. Otherwise, you're making faces in a vacuum.

LEE J. COBB:
> When you're young, you look for the romance in acting. You set out to slay the dragon. . . . It isn't until later, much later, when you're in it and it's too late to get out, that the romance flies out the window.

JAMES COBURN:
> People like to think of you as that great superhuman figure on the screen doing all those giant things. In the end, a lot of actors get to thinking they are like that. First we've got to learn to be human beings—we mustn't just be our profession.

CLAUDETTE COLBERT:
> Why didn't I make more films? Because there have been no offers.

JUDY COLLINS:
> The fantasy world of stardom is cheating us all out of our lives.

RONALD COLMAN:
> I wish I might find a Shangri-La.

BETTY COMPSON:
> Nothing really serious—just like the sailors: I have a sweetheart in every part.

SEAN CONNERY:
> I'm not mean, I'm Scottish.

> The proper sadist is always aware of what he's doing.

CHUCK CONNORS:
> I don't want my kids to grow up believing that there is nothing

destructive in the world. I want them to know that there is good and bad in the world, that you can be hurt physically, that guns can kill you, that drugs are bad for you, that not everyone means well.

JACKIE COOGAN:
All actors are really crazy.

GARY COOPER:
Everybody asks me, "How come you're around so long?" Well, I always attribute it to playing the part of Mr. Average Joe American. Just an average guy from the middle of the USA. And then, I guess I got to believe it... Gary Cooper, an Average Charlie, who became a movie actor.

JACKIE COOPER:
My whole life I've been trying to prove I'm not just yesterday. The whole child-star situation can become a demon walking along with you.

BILL COSBY, on racial stereotypes and typecasting:
I don't sing, tap dance, juggle, or say "Sir."

JOSEPH COTTEN:
Movies and the theater aren't life. They're only part of it. We make a living out of acting and pray we don't get associated with too much junk.

...but, in the end, all we hope to reach is a high standard of compromise.

NOËL COWARD:
Good heavens, television is something you appear on; you don't watch.

TONY CURTIS:
I hope that in a few years I'll have enough security so I can drive around in an old battered station wagon if I want to.

All you have to do is know your lines. What you have to avoid is acting.

I educated my fans. They began to say to themselves, "Well, Burt Lancaster don't play scenes with bums."

LINDA DARNELL:
I am told when surface beauty is gone, the real woman emerges.

DANIELLE DARRIEUX:
The stage takes more from your life in three hours of work than one whole day in the film studio. On stage, you are a prisoner, even though it is a lovely prison.

MARION DAVIES, comedienne and mistress of William Randolph Hearst:

With me, it was five per cent talent and ninety-five per cent publicity.

What's wrong with kissing? Germs?

Hearst come, Hearst served.

SAMMY DAVIS, JR.:

A black person never leaves the ghetto.

I'm a colored, one-eyed Jew—do I need anything else?

Complete ugliness, utter ugliness, like mine, though, is most attractive. Yes, yes, I'm convinced that a really ugly man, in the end, seems attractive.

SAMMY DAVIS 1959

DORIS DAY:

I've always thought that God meant for us to be in twos like the animals in the ark.

It's my cameraman who is getting older.

JAMES DEAN:

I act for the same reason most actors act, to express the fantasies in which I have involved myself.

OLIVIA DE HAVILLAND:

The camera is pitiless.

Women have always been afraid of being hurt.

One must take what comes, with laughter.

Life is a movie too.

ALAIN DELON:

In my office in Paris, I have a photograph of the earth taken from the moon. . . . It helps me have the right values. I may be a great big moviestar down here, but from up there I am nothing, and we are all nothing.

I am not a star. I am an actor. I have been fighting for ten years to make people forget that I am just a pretty boy with a beautiful face. It's a hard fight, but I will win it.

Next to being an actor, I would have enjoyed being a gangster.

CATHERINE DENEUVE:

All men are Arabs.

I don't want to be possessed.

ROBERT DE NIRO:

I don't want people to recognize me when I walk in the streets.

You have to earn the right to play a character.

KIRK DOUGLAS:

I just want. . . to help people forget their own problems and to get lost in the problems of the people on the screen. Isn't that what going to the movies is all about?

Virtue isn't photogenic.

I've finally got away from Burt Lancaster. My luck has changed for the better. I've got nice-looking girls in my films now.

My life is a B movie. . .the typical American success story is a B movie.

MELVYN DOUGLAS:

I earned what became an international reputation for being one of the most debonair and witty farceurs in Hollywood.

RICHARD DREYFUSS:

You know why I got so many dates? Because I have a forty-foot face.

KEIR DULLEA:

Oh, if only I had a wrinkle or two!

FAYE DUNAWAY:
It's the plight of the beautiful woman. The world accepts you for your looks, expects you to behave a certain way, to create a certain image. If you don't force the world to stop tugging at you, after a while you stop knowing the difference between who you really are and who they demand you must be.

JIMMY DURANTE:
Be nice to people on your way up because you meet 'em on your way down.

CLINT EASTWOOD:
Actually I'm eighteen. I've just lived hard.

The self-sufficient human being is become a mythological character in our day and age.

There's nothing wrong with glamorizing the gun.

ANITA EKBERG:
You don't need nudity. A real actress should have her clothes on. Besides, you should leave something to the imagination.

BRITT EKLAND:
I'm very careful to look beautiful when people photograph me.

DAME EDITH EVANS:
People always ask me the most ridiculous questions. They want to know, "How do you approach a role?" Well, I don't know. I approach it by first saying yes, then getting on with the bloody thing.

FRANÇOISE FABIAN, French actress:
Affairs don't need a pretext. They start with a look and end with breakfast.

PETER FALK:
It took me nine years to get married, ten to become an actor.

MIA FARROW:
If I weren't doing what I'm doing now, the actress thing, the star business, if you want to call it that, whatever it is, I'd be in an asylum. I'm sure of it.

I can match bottoms with anyone in Hollywood.

ALICE FAYE:
What did I have? I don't know. Maybe it was the girl-next-door, the one you left behind. It was wartime.

I don't live in the past, but the old movies are still the ones people remember. I watch them on TV and cry like a slob.

PETER FINCH:

I've grown accustomed to my face, as the song goes, and, I gather, so have film producers. Others call it either aristocratic or baggy...you can call it sex appeal. I call it a character-filled face that has lived.

ALBERT FINNEY:

Now that I can afford all the shirts I want, I find people in shops insist I have them as a present.

GERALDINE FITZGERALD, with a rueful comment on the Hollywood of the Forties:

We were like pawns in a game of chess; we were permitted to move in only one direction. Only queens could move in all directions.

RHONDA FLEMING, on matrimony:

Till then, no one had said the magic words, "Quit working," in that sweet, sweet way.

ERROL FLYNN:

I won't be content until I can live a free life—do the things I want to do, when I want to do them....

I want to be taken seriously...I allow myself to be understood abroad as a colorful fragment in a drab world.

One thing I always knew how to do: enjoy life. If I have any genius, it is a genius for living.

Mostly, I walked through my pictures.

A star doesn't have to pursue or seduce any woman. What he needs, more likely, is a chastity belt for self-protection, as some of my movie pals will tell you.

The rest of my life will be devoted to women and litigation.

Son, it isn't what they say about you—it's what they whisper about you.

NINA FOCH:

When I'm cleaning around the house I wear an apron, but nothing else. It makes my activities—dusting, washing—more interesting to my husband.

HENRY FONDA:

Acting is putting on a mask. The worst torture that can happen to me is not having a mask to get in back of.

I do what John Ford tells me to do.

JANE FONDA:

I found out that acting was hell. You spend all your time trying to do what they put people in asylums for.

Hollywood's wonderful. They pay you for making love.

Working in Hollywood does give one a certain expertise in the field of prostitution.

Life is not Hollywood.

PETER FONDA:

It is my responsibility to spread the truth. Within me I find the problems of the world.

AVA GARDNER:

Deep down, I'm pretty superficial.

I made it as a star dressed. If I haven't got it dressed, I don't want it.

I don't remember how many swimsuits I wore out—without getting near the water. I shot enough sultry looks around the MGM photo gallery to melt the North Pole.

If people making a movie didn't keep kissing, they'd be at each other's throats.

There comes a time when you've got to face the fact that you're an old broad.

JAMES GARNER:

They've taken all the magic out of motion pictures. The mystery's gone.

GREER GARSON:

Even when a petal falls from a rose, it keeps me awake.

VITTORIO GASSMAN:

I've made fifty-five movies. I'd say forty of them were dreadful, and the four I made in Hollywood were probably the most dreadful of all.

JANET GAYNOR:

What do you mean, comeback? I was always on top.

I enjoyed it all and have no sad tales to tell you.

BEN GAZZARA:

You go through a kind of honeymoon when you make a movie, being in very close contact with the same people for a long time. After that you go back to your own life.

SIR JOHN GIELGUD:

What is it that makes the so-called "star." Energy, an athletic voice, a well-graced manner, certainty of execution, some unusually fascinating originality of temperament? Vitality, certainly, and the ability to convey the impression of beauty and ugliness as the part demands, as well as authority and a sense of style.

HERMIONE GINGOLD:

Never marry or even dally with a Scandinavian—it's the latitude.

I got all the schooling an actress needs. That is, I learned to write enough to sign contracts.

PAULETTE GODDARD:

I am not temperamental. I just know what I want, and if I don't have it, I try to get it.

RUTH GORDON:

Anything that begins "I don't know how to tell you this" is never good news.

BETTY GRABLE:

If I was sexy, I was just being me.

I'm a truck driver's delight.

STEWART GRANGER:

Acting now bores the hell out of me. I know I haven't a nutshell of talent compared to my wife, Jean Simmons.

LEE GRANT:

Cute is good. . .being young is absolutely essential.

PETER GRAVES:

Once the motion pictures straighten themselves out, the first girl to make three good pictures in a row will be a star.

HANK GREENBERG:

I'm a B player. I can't beat the good guys, but I'm good enough to play with them.

ANDY GRIFFITH:

What I like is to play a character like me.

CORINNE GRIFFITH:

Why should I go on until I am playing mother roles? I have plenty of money. I want to improve my mind. Most of the time you'll find me bobbing around in Europe.

⸱⸱N GRUEN:

I have always considered anyone who denied wanting to be a star a bare-faced liar. As for me, I am pure as the driven snow, guileless as a child, and completely serious—I want to be a star.

ALEC GUINNESS:
> I don't really know who I am. Quite possibly, I do not exist at all.

GENE HACKMAN:
> Seventy-five per cent of being successful as an actor is pure luck—the rest is just endurance.

ANN HARDING:
> I don't want to look like an actress, I want to look like a person.

SIR CEDRIC HARDWICKE:
> Actors and burglars work better at night.

RICHARD HARRIS:
> No actor—I don't care whether he's Richard Burton or Laurence Olivier—can act pain. You have to actually suffer to make it look authentic.

> You can sum up my life and my acting in one sentence: "I want to play all the strings in the bow, because I want to find out how many strings there are. . . ."

REX HARRISON:
> I have never regretted the choice of any parts I have done. Because you get involved in the part, you grow to love the character, and you can never regret something you love.

LAURENCE HARVEY:
> Some of my best moments are spent with me.

JUNE HAVER, summing up her career:
> I had ten good years in the movies.

JACK HAWKINS, who lost the use of his own voice:
> I would like some very bright spark to invent silent movies.

GOLDIE HAWN:
> In the new contract, I get offices. I mean, Goldie Hawn has offices at Universal, isn't that insane?

STERLING HAYDEN, in an anti-Hollywood mood:
> I'm leaving this turmoil for the tranquility of war.

HELEN HAYES:
> In the theater, you have a special audience; you can switch back and forth from "good" people to "bad" people and get away with it. On the screen, the public somehow wants to accept you the way they see you. You acquire a certain image for them.

> An actress' life is so transitory—suddenly you're a building.

RITA HAYWORTH:

When you're in love, you're living, you matter.

Every man I've known has fallen in love with Gilda and wakened with me.

EILEEN HECKART:

I don't feel the need to be a star. I can walk freely through a supermarket without being stopped for my autograph. That's just fine.

MARGAUX HEMINGWAY:

Men are six feet, women are five feet twelve.

DAVID HEMMINGS:

Here I am living like this, flying from one country to another, eating in marvellous restaurants, living in super luxury. What a lucky thing to have happened!

SONJA HENIE, skating star:

Count the house while you're spinning around.

Jewellery takes people's minds off your wrinkles.

AUDREY HEPBURN:

Whatever happens, the most important thing is growing old gracefully. And you can't do that on the cover of a fan magazine.

CHARLTON HESTON:

I don't seem to have a Twentieth Century face.

If you can't make a career out of two DeMilles, you'll never make it.

Nudity is never erotic, except in the bedroom.

ANNE HEYWOOD:

In America, if you're demure, they think you are just dumb.

DUSTIN HOFFMAN:

I always used to think I wanted to be an actor, when all along what I really wanted, deep down, was to be a movie star. It's something you just don't admit, even to yourself.

I do have this terrible suspicion that if I play myself I'm going to be bloody boring.

WILLIAM HOLDEN:

I found the greatest sleeping pill in the world: this script.

I like to think of emotions as being a series of cloaks hung on pegs; I take them down as I find I need them.

Frankenstein *and* My Fair Lady *are really the same story.*

JUDY HOLLIDAY:

I seem to be blessed with fine pumice somewhere around my vocal cords.

Sometimes, when I'm trying to do a scene, I get terribly aware of myself. I see myself doing it. That's no good. It's like self-sabotage.

CELESTE HOLM:

Acting is controlled schizophrenia. That sounds neurotic but isn't. You are playing someone else while being yourself.

BOB HOPE, on a dud picture:

When they catch John Dillinger, they're going to make him sit through it twice.

TREVOR HOWARD:

"Faking" is the proper work for acting.

LESLIE HOWARD:

I haven't the slightest intention of playing another weak, watery character such as Ashley Wilkes. I've played enough ineffectual characters already.

ROCK HUDSON:
> The only thing I can say in my defence is that I did the best I could. It was pretty rotten, I agree, but it was my best.

> I need a script to order a sandwich.

KIM HUNTER:
> Whatever the technique, your aim must always be to achieve command over the audience.

TAB HUNTER:
> I'm typical of where publicity is a zillion years ahead of career.

WALTER HUSTON:
> Son, always give 'em a good show, and travel first class!

BETTY HUTTON:
> Nobody loved me unless I bought them, and so I bought everybody.

WILFRID HYDE-WHITE:
> They sent Oscar Wilde, that poor man, to Reading Jail for doing what all other actors today get knighted for.

REX INGRAM:
> There are no bad actors, only bad directors.

SAM JAFFE:
> A picture pulling in twenty million dollars is making a mess of money.

GLENDA JACKSON:
> Being nominated for an Oscar is like being pregnant with a child someone else may have for all your labor pains.

> I've always thought that I'm not pretty enough to be thought beautiful, and not quite plain enough to be considered interesting.

> I can't actually see myself putting make-up on my face at the age of sixty. But I can see myself going on a camel train to Samarkand.

GLYNIS JOHNS:
> I have not enjoyed being a star. It has made me ill, exhausted, and unhappy.

VAN JOHNSON:
> A man just gets to his beautiful period when he is forty.

JENNIFER JONES:
> I don't know what to say to people when they start telling me what a great actress I am!

DANNY KAYE:
> *If there is a dispute between a musician and myself, it is settled amicably. I win.*

DIANE KEATON:
> *If you really don't like publicity, you don't decide to become an actress. It goes with the territory.*

> *I'm glad I'm alive.*

DEBORAH KERR:
> *The camera always seems to find an innate gentility in me.*

EVELYN KEYES:
> *I have often wondered what would have happened to me if I had needed a size 38 bra instead of a modest 34.*

MARGOT KIDDER, about her appearance in *Playboy:*
> *If you're fourteen and reading this, take solace: You probably look a lot better than you think. And nobody looks like Miss January.*

EARTHA KITT:
> *You don't have to hit anybody on the head with four-letter words to be sexy.*

JACK KLUGMAN:
> *All acting is remembering what you did on the stage.*

HILDEGARD KNEF:
> *Paradise has palm trees.*

ALEXANDER KNOX:
> *On the stage and on the screen there are two kinds of actors: actors who behave and actors who act.*

ALAN LADD:
> *My career? I was kept busy. Isn't that enough?*

VERONICA LAKE:
> *If I had stayed in Hollywood I would have ended up like Alan Ladd and Gail Russell—dead and buried by now.*

> *I wanted to reach up on the screen and yank that hair back from the girl's eye.*

> *Veronica Lake is a Hollywood creation. Hollywood is good at doing that sort of thing.*

HEDY LAMARR:
> *If you use your imagination, you can look at any actress and see her nude. I hope to make you use your imagination.*

I thought with some interesting make-up, a sarong and some hip-swinging, I would make a memorable nymphomaniac.

Any girl can be glamorous. All you have to do is stand still and look stupid.

I win because I learned years ago that scared money always loses. I never care, so I win.

I was the highest-priced and most important star in Hollywood, but I was "difficult."

To be a star is to own the world and all the people in it. After a taste of stardom, everything else is poverty.

FERNANDO LAMAS:
I got into movies because it was a great way to meet broads.

BURT LANCASTER:
Once the public decides what you are, you might as well give up trying to be anything else.

I guess I'm the guy who always went to bed with the girl—even if it was only after the movie had finished.

ELSA LANCHESTER:
One thinks of a film star as a kind of gaily colored bird, forever giving itself a final preening under the bright lights. Whereas it's all hard work, aspirins, and usually purgatives.

CAROLE LANDIS:
I was ex-wifed to death. It might be the husband's fault, you know.

ANGELA LANSBURY:
We all need someone to tell us, "Yes, you can do it."

One day I was making $18 a week at Bullock's department store, and the next day I was up to $500 a week at MGM.

Let's face it. I've finally arrived.

MARIO LANZA:
Reality stinks most of the time. It's a star's duty to take people out of the world of reality into the world of illusion, and a motion picture is the ideal way to do that.

CHARLES LAUGHTON:
But they can't censor the gleam in my eye.

PETER LAWFORD, on the star system:
I never did become the next Ronald Colman.

If you survived, you were a star.

BRUCE LEE:
> If I hadn't become a star, I would probably have ended up a gangster.

JANET LEIGH:
> People tell me often that I express a spirit of happiness. They do, really! And this makes me very glad. Because it means I have such a great opportunity to give!

VIVIEN LEIGH:
> Most of us have compromised with life. Those who fight for what they want will always thrill us.
>
> I never liked Scarlett. I knew it was a marvellous part, but I never cared for her.

JACK LEMMON:
> Suddenly you find that you're only giving two performances a year. You're a success as an actor, but vast limitations have been placed on your work. If you defy the system—take a character role, as many fine actors in England do—then you're not a star any more, and the best pictures won't be offered to you.

LOTTA LENYA:
> The New York skyline was as familiar as Berlin's. We'd seen it so many times in the movies.
>
> And you learn how to settle for what you get.

OSCAR LEVANT, wit, pianist and professional hypochondriac:
> My health is a thing of national concern.
>
> My behavior has been impeccable; I've been unconscious for the past six months.
>
> I drink only to make other people interesting.
>
> People either dislike or detest me.

VIVECA LINDFORS:
> Actresses get most of their work between the ages of eighteen and thirty, when they know the least.

GINA LOLLOBRIGIDA:
> I get very irritated when people think I must be the same women I portray on the screen.

CAROLE LOMBARD:
> When you're in there fighting, you always feel so clean. Ugly things drop away.
>
> I can't call my soul my own—I have no say about my own business. Lincoln freed the slaves, but he didn't know about me at the time.

Hollywood is where they write the alibis before they write the story.

SOPHIA LOREN:

Acting and living are quite close. You grow as an actress when you grow as a person. The first essential for an actress is to seem human.

Sex appeal is fifty per cent what you've got and fifty per cent what people think you've got.

Everything you see I owe to spaghetti.

PETER LORRE:

All you need to imitate me is a pair of soft-boiled eggs and a bedroom voice.

LINDA LOVELACE:

If you don't have an orgasm daily, you become very nervous, very uptight. I do, anyway.

MYRNA LOY:

They say the movies should be more like life—I think life should be more like the movies.

BELA LUGOSI:

In Hungary acting is a profession. In America it is a decision.

ALFRED LUNT, on acting and dancing:

I speak in a loud, clear voice, and try not to bump into the furniture.

MERCEDES McCAMBRIDGE:

If there is such a thing as reincarnation, I would like to come back as James Dean.

LEO McCAREY:

I never made a picture yet that fell off the screen.

JOEL McCREA:

Acting? I Never attempt it. A placid sort of fellow, that's me...so when I face the cameras, I just stay placid.

If I hadn't become an actor, I'd have been a cattleman all my life.

ALI MacGRAW:

This success thing is all a little scary.

SHIRLEY MacLAINE:

In front of the cameras I have to be careful what I think because it all shows.

I lost to a tracheotomy.

STEVE McQUEEN:
> The world is as good as you are. You've got to learn to like yourself first.

ANNA MAGNANI:
> It's so unfair that we should die just because we are born.

MARJORIE MAIN, on her best-remembered role:
> I always thought of Ma Kettle as a real person—someone I could drive out into the country and see.

JAYNE MANSFIELD:
> I love candlelight, music, artistic things, squirrels, and rabbits, my Great Dane, and my pink Jaguar.

> I'm trying to appear casual. I want people to think I'm used to mink.

> I got married, and we had a baby nine months and ten seconds later.

> Men are those creatures with two legs and eight hands.

FREDRIC MARCH:
> Keep interested in others; keep interested in the wide and wonderful world. Then, in a spiritual sense, you will always be young.

> Let me confirm that I have definitely retired. Not, however, as definitely as James Cagney.

DEAN MARTIN:
> I would become governor only if all the drunks voted for me.

> Any bum who can't get drunk by midnight ain't trying.

> The only reason I drink is because when I am sober I think I am Eddie Fisher.

LEE MARVIN:
> One of the good things about getting older is that you find you're more interesting than most of the people you meet.

> Love is a matter of degrees. I think of a gas tank with the empty and full positions.

JAMES MASON:
> I'm tired of playing the lecherous, middle-aged chap who is forever vaulting the generation gap.

> I think the question people should ask is, "Of all your films, which is the one you'd like most to have destroyed?"

RAYMOND MASSEY:
> When you have to please Kansas City and Kensington, and try to do both at once, the ultimate product cannot help but be mediocre.

MARCELLO MASTROIANNI:

They come for you in the morning in a limousine; they take you to the studio; they stick a pretty girl in your arms; sometimes they earn something off you and give you some of the profits. They call that a profession? Come on!

I love and adore my wife, and I equally adore Catherine Deneuve.

VICTOR MATURE:

Actually, I am a golfer. That is my real occupation. I never was an actor; ask anybody, particularly the critics.

MELINA MERCOURI:

Men. Let's start with men.

BURGESS MEREDITH:

You have to act with joy, and not mislocate the center of the emotions, which is in the head, not in the stomach. The center of the emotions is right above the eyes.

SARAH MILES:

There's a little bit of hooker in very woman. A little bit of hooker and a little bit of God.

RAY MILLAND:

...good acting. It exhilarates me and robs me of sleep.

My granny used to say, "The truth can always hurt, be careful with it."

ANN MILLER:

As an actress I'm terrible...but if Ava Gardner and Lana Turner can act under a good director, I think I have still got a chance.

YVETTE MIMEUX:

I'm five-feet-four, but I always feel six-foot-one, tall and strong.

LIZA MINNELLI:

I look like a female Fred Astaire.

MARY MILNES MINTER:

I do not care for any praise but that of my mother.

ROBERT MITCHUM:

You know something? What I represent to the public is hope. They look at me and they think: If that big slob can get somewhere, there's a chance for us.

Listen, I got three expressions: looking left, looking right, and looking straight ahead.

I've never been an actor—and I've got seventy movies to prove it.

MARIA MONTEZ:

My peectures are getting nakeder and nakeder.

My legs are so good pipple theenk they must be American.

Each time I look in mirror, I vant to scream; I am so beautiful.

ROBERT MONTGOMERY:

My advice to you concerning applause is this: Enjoy it but never quite believe it.

COLLEEN MOORE:

"Oh, if only I was a star!" the girls used to say. I never said that. I said, "When I'm a star...."

ROGER MOORE:

I replace everyone. I'll be replacing Mickey Mouse in about three years' time.

AGNES MOOREHEAD:

The trick is to be the best maid or cook or spear-carrier that you can.

JEANNE MOREAU:

Most people don't have the energy for true passion, so they give up and go to the movies.

Age does not protect you from love. But love, to some extent, protects you from age.

To age well it helps to have two things: fame and money.

ROBERT MORLEY, well-girthed actor:

I still think it is wonderful that I can make people pay to see me act.

My future is safe in three-dimensional films.

PAUL MUNI:

The man who never made an enemy never made anything.

CONRAD NAGEL:

I don't enjoy seeing myself on the late-late shows because I get mad that I'm not being paid for them now.

PATRICIA NEAL:

Happy? Who's really happy? Let's say it is enough not to be unhappy and let it go at that.

PAUL NEWMAN:

My own personality is so vapid and bland, I have to go steal the personalities of other people to be effective on the screen.

I have often thought it might very well appear in my obituary or on my tombstone or somewhere that "Here lies Paul Newman who died a complete failure because his eyes suddenly turned brown."

JACK NICHOLSON:

I remember that someone once said that the whole thing is to keep working, and pretty soon they'll think you're good.

LEONARD NIMOY:

If I am not Spock, who is?

DAVID NIVEN:

I do only one movie a year, and after each I am convinced nobody is going to ask me to do another.

Print anything you like, and I'll swear I said it.

I once described my face as a cross between two pound's of halibut and an explosion in an old clothes closet.

KIM NOVAK:

There is a hopeless poison that gets into actresses when they become big stars.

MERLE OBERON:

Without security it is difficult for a woman to look or feel beautiful.

HUGH O'BRIAN:

I hate that word "star." Do you know what "star" spells backwards? "Rats."

MAUREEN O'HARA:

I don't object to being called The Queen of Technicolor.

PETER O'TOOLE:

I was sort of the Vanessa Redgrave of the Fifties.

AL PACINO:

I don't need any bodyguards. I'm from the South Bronx.

An actor becomes an emotional athlete. You work on yourself as an instrument.

GERALDINE PAGE:

We wouldn't want to know the people we go to see on the stage. How would you like to have Medea for dinner? Or Macbeth slurping your soup? Or Oedipus with his bloody, blinded eyes dripping all over your tablecloth?

IRENE PAPAS:

Wherever I am is Greece...I carry it with me wherever I go.

SUZY PARKER:
An American girl is against everything a Frenchman stands for.

ANN PENNINGTON:
I'd rather be thought of as the way I used to be.

ANTHONY PERKINS:
One of my stage directors taught me that the best acting is spare acting, the sparest, with the smallest gesture, the greatest economy. I've learned how to mete it out.

VALERIE PERRINE:
A girl with large breasts has two strikes against her.

JEAN PETERS:
We need people to personify our dreams.

DONALD PLEASANCE:
There comes a moment on-stage when you can't deny yourself, and you can't deny the part you are playing. Somehow these two things come together when you act.

SIDNEY POITIER:
I'm an American, first and foremost. Then, I'm an actor. Finally, if you like, I'm a Negro.

JANE POWELL:
I think now I've found my own happy ending without the help of a script.

TYRONE POWER:
I've done an awful lot of stuff that's a monument to public patience.

ELVIS PRESLEY:
I'm going to buy a castle and live like any other GI.

ROBERT PRESTON:
Next to acting myself, watching other actors gives me my greatest joy.

VINCENT PRICE:
One great actor of the past labelled himself and his fellow actors as "sculptors in snow."

ANTHONY QUAYLE:
If you're an actor, you walk a tightrope between two extremes, between justifiable pride and humility. You have to cultivate a complete carelessness of yourself, in a way, or else become an egotistical, introspective monster.

ANTHONY QUINN:

On the stage, you have to find the truth, even if you have to lose the audience.

In Europe, an actor is an artist. In Hollywood, if he isn't working, he's a bum.

GEORGE RAFT, who played and, in real life, associated with gangsters:

My name was Ranft but I dropped the "n" because Raft was easier to pronounce. My father never forgave me for that.

What have I got to do to clear myself? I lead a quiet life. I don't ask for any trouble. I have never taken a drink. I don't get in any fights. If broads are an offence, then I plead guilty.

LUISE RAINER:

My dreams? All my dreams are dreams of fear.

TONY RANDALL:

Compassion is a luxury of the affluent.

BASIL RATHBONE:

My secret is a woman. She is small. She is vital. She has red hair. Her name is Ouida. She is my wife.

RONALD REAGAN:

I did a string of pictures with the Dead End Kids, which was an experience similar to going over Niagara Falls in a barrel the hard way—upstream.

I enjoyed every whizzing minute of it.

ROBERT REDFORD:

I'm Robert Redford only when I'm alone.

LYNN REDGRAVE:

The only difference between Vanessa and me is six years of age and one inch of height.

MICHAEL REDGRAVE:

Hollywood was all right for three months.

VANESSA REDGRAVE:

Films are where the art and excitement are today. And being a movie star—it's super.

OLIVER REED:

Do you know what I am? I'm successful. Destroy me and you destroy the British film industry. Keep me going and I'm the biggest star you've got. I'm Mr. England.

WALLACE REID:

Just between you and me I'd like to do something worth while some day—give something to the world beside my face and figure.

LEE REMICK:

I'm not a martyr to truth. I play within my own limits.

Everyone has a false image of himself. When I first saw myself on the screen, twenty-five-feet tall, what I saw was so unexpected that I couldn't look at anyone else in the picture.

You are your own instrument.

LIZ RENAY:

Life for me begins with every sunrise.

BURT REYNOLDS:

You always think there is something interesting inside a wall safe.

I'm finally getting scripts that don't have Steve McQueen's fingerprints all over them.

DEBBIE REYNOLDS:

It's very hard to climb the ladder, and it's very easy to go down the slide.

SIR RALPH RICHARDSON:

The art of acting consists of keeping people from coughing.

RACHEL ROBERTS:

I used to be a very good actress. Then I married Rex Harrison and got lost...I couldn't live on one more yacht for one more day.

CLIFF ROBERTSON:

This isn't exactly a stable business. It's like trying to stand up in a canoe with your pants down.

PAUL ROBESON:

I thought I could do something for the Negro race in films, show the truth about them and other people, too.

EDWARD G. ROBINSON:

Nature gives every man a face of his own.

MICKEY ROONEY:

I'm the only man who has a marriage licence made out To Whom It May Concern.

I have so many wives and so many children I don't know whom to visit at Christmas time.

I was a fourteen-year-old boy for thirty years.

JANE RUSSELL:
Sometimes the photographers would pose me in a low-necked nightgown and tell me to bend down and pick up the pails. They were not shooting the pails.

ROSALIND RUSSELL:
I was always the threat, you see, to all the great women stars at Metro, and they certainly were legion.

Quality is important in everything, and it pays, pays and pays.

Success is a public affair. Failure is a private funeral.

EVA MARIE SAINT, accepting an Academy Award:
All I can say after that is "Oh, shit!"

JILL ST. JOHN:
I was a woman at six.

GEORGE SANDERS:
An actor is not quite a human being—but then, who is?

I am content with mediocrity.

Whereas on the screen I am invariably a sonofabitch, in life I am a dear, dear boy.

Sanders took his own life, leaving this note:

Dear World, I am leaving because I am bored. I feel I have lived long enough. I am leaving you with your worries in this sweet cesspool—good luck.

MARIA SCHELL:
A great film always has the flavor of its country.

MAXIMILIAN SCHELL:
I always said I won't marry until I go to Japan and see the beautiful women there. I've been to Japan now, and I have to have another excuse.

There are two souls in every actor. One watches the other. When both are content at the same time, you have a good moment.

JOSEPH SCHILDKRAUT:
The American man dies sixteen deaths inside him before he says "I love you."

MARIA SCHNEIDER:
> I learned not from the studio but from the streets.

PAUL SCOFIELD:
> Magic is for the audience to discover. Magic is no concern of ours.

GEORGE C. SCOTT:
> I mean, don't you think it's a pretty spooky way to earn a living?

> The essence of art should be life and change—and that can't be where films are concerned. The film freezes your art forever. No matter how much better you become, there is no way to improve the performance you've done for the camera. It's locked. And there's a certain, sad death in that.

> After a while the pleasure stops, but the self-contempt stays.

LIZABETH SCOTT:
> I'm in love with a wonderful life; a life of living alone.

JEAN SEBERG:
> Sometimes I wonder why people go on acting, exposing the most secret things about themselves.

> A movie studio is your friend until you're crippled.

GEORGE SEGAL:
> The good thing about the movies is that you can eat and meditate at the same time.

> Paul Newman is the last star. He's the link. We're just actors.

OMAR SHARIF:
> I love sex, wine, and food—after a hard day's work, they are my rewards.

NORMA SHEARER:
> In a picture things are made to work out.

> I suddenly found myself feeling that life is very short and that we simply have to live it as best we can.

CYBILL SHEPHERD:
> When you finally catch on to the fact that most men aren't interested in what you have to say—and are only looking at you because you're pretty—it's a big shock.

DINAH SHORE:
> I never thought I was photogenic. I thought I looked terrible on the Technicolor screen.

JEAN SHRIMPTON:
> *I think it's rather good that the public loses interest...I think that's healthy.*

SYLVIA SIDNEY, on her Hollywood years:
> *It was a dream world, a kind of Alice in Wonderland, with its kings and queens, princes and princesses, and our millions of loyal subjects. But it wasn't real, and it couldn't last.*

SIMONE SIGNORET:
> *The body of an actor is like a well in which experiences are stored, then tapped when needed.*

PHIL SILVERS:
> *I've never won an interview yet.*

PENNY SINGLETON:
> *I'm not as young as my teeth or as old as my tongue.*

WALTER SLEZAK, on a sneak preview that went very badly:
> *We had two thousand deaf-mute Albanians out front tonight. How were yours?*

BARBARA STANWYCK:
> *Put me in the last fifteen minutes of a picture, and I don't care what happened before. I don't even care if I was in the rest of the damn thing—I'll take it in those fifteen minutes.*
>
> *All I want, all any of the real pros want, is a decent script, a competent cast, and a good director. The rest is a crock of shit.*

MAUREEN STAPLETON:
> *Actors are a much hardier breed of people than any other people. We have to be as clever as rats to survive.*

ROD STEIGER:
> *All artists have the one quality that is priceless—eternal childhood.*
>
> *The actor reminds people of the poetry of being alive.*

INGER STEVENS:
> *Children are no different from other people. They're just shorter.*

STELLA STEVENS:
> *Working as an actress they always wanted me as a dumb sexy blonde, and that was easy enough.*

JAMES STEWART:
> *The secret of a happy life is to accept change gracefully.*

BARBRA STREISAND:

I'm terribly lazy. That's why I love being in movies. I'm performing all over the world—while I'm home taking a bath.

You can't eat more than one pastrami-on-rye sandwich at a time.

You think beautiful girls are going to stay in style forever?

ELAINE STRITCH:

Everybody's afraid. Couples who've been married for thirty years wake up in a cold sweat.... I sometimes wonder if some of my married friends don't ask me to come around—alone—to sing for my supper and give 'em a lot of laughs—so they won't have to cope with each other.

MARGARET SULLAVAN:

Perhaps I'll get used to the bizarre, elaborate theatricalism called Hollywood, but I cannot guarantee it.

DONALD SUTHERLAND:

As an actor, you can only bring so much to a film. As a director, there is almost no limit.

An actor is successful when he can create a character with the minimum of gesture and words. That is what I strive for.

ROBERT TAYLOR:

I've never been terribly ambitious—simply wanted to do a good job at whatever I did. The reviews usually said I gave an adequate or good performance. I never got raves, but neither did I get pans. I've never had an Oscar and probably never will. I'm content to try to do as well as I can.

DAME MARIE TEMPEST:

I never allow myself to be bored, because boredom is aging. If you live in the past you grow old, and dull, and dusty. It's very nice, of course, to be young and beautiful; but there are other qualities, thank God.

SHIRLEY TEMPLE:

I class myself with Rin Tin Tin. People were looking for something to cheer them up. They fell in love with a dog and a little girl.

I remember when I was three and unknown....

DANNY THOMAS:

I don't think it's necessary for talented people to show their bodies on the screen...I think it will be exciting some day if a picture begins with a nude person who's putting his clothes on, and keeps them on for the rest of the picture.

With my nose, they'll think I'm Jewish.

GENE TIERNEY:

I had no trouble playing any kind of role. My problems began when I had to be myself.

FRANCHOT TONE:

I'm not saying I was too courageous to quit. But at least I was too stubborn.

CHAIM TOPOL:

In our country, Israel, we don't believe in miracles. We rely on them.

JOHN TRAVOLTA:

A confirmed bachelor is a guy who believes in wine, women, and so long. I'm a confirmed bachelor.

JEAN-LOUIS TRINTIGNANT:

The best actor in the world is the one who feels the most and shows the least.

LANA TURNER:

Whenever I do something, it seems so right. And turns out so wrong.

How does it happen that something that makes so much sense in the moonlight doesn't make any sense at all in the sunlight?

Of the deglamorization of the film world she said:

Give the people back their dreams. It's tough enough as it is.

LIV ULLMANN:

Something has to be kept for the person I'm with. My breasts aren't actresses.

Reality can be magnificent even when life is not.

PETER USTINOV:

If Botticelli were alive today, he'd be working for Vogue.

No! I'm the star. In this scene I do nothing.

JON VOIGHT:

The only thing that should be taken seriously is a reverence for humanity, crazy humanity.

JOHNNY WEISSMULLER:

I don't mind if they keep pointing at me and saying, "Hey, him Tarzan!" I love it.

The main thing is not to let go of the vine.

RAQUEL WELCH:

There aren't any hard women, only soft men.

The mind can also be an erogenous zone.

TUESDAY WELD:

It seems the brighter you are, the deeper the hole you get into.

OSKAR WERNER:

The things we do are never more than the shadows of our dreams.

RICHARD WIDMARK:

They think you're playing yourself. The truth is that the only person who can ever really play himself is a baby.

The whole thing fell apart when they started calling movies film.

I've played nine million generals.

MICHAEL WILDING:

You can pick out actors by the glazed look that comes into their eyes when the conversation wanders away from themselves.

ESTHER WILLIAMS:

All they ever did for me at MGM was to change my leading men and the water in the pool.

NICOL WILLIAMSON:

I love to dare.

SHELLEY WINTERS:

In Hollywood all marriages are happy. It's trying to live together afterward that causes the problems.

NATALIE WOOD:

You get tough in this business, until you get big enough to hire people to get tough for you. Then you can sit back and be a lady.

JOANNE WOODWARD:

The real me is all the parts I've played!

JANE WYMAN:

I won this Oscar by keeping my mouth shut. I think I'll do it again.

KEENAN WYNN:

In our profession, there are a lot of people, but few actors.

SUSANNAH YORK:

Once you stop feeling that you're discovering things, then you will know that you're at the end, so far as being a creative artist is concerned.

LORETTA YOUNG:

If you want a place in he sun, you have to expect a few blisters.

5
Feature Presentations

In the pages that follow, the leads are played by the stars of five ever-popular film genres. Screen comedy, which grew out of vaudeville and into films through mime, is the subject of "You'll Laugh, You'll Cry." Musicals came into their own with the talkies and are featured in "Musical Extravaganzas." Westerns, as old as the motion picture industry itself, are presented in "Horse Operas." Horror films, a staple of screen entertainment, are considered in "Shivers and Shrieks." We close with the sex symbols presenting their side of the battle of the sexes in "Love Goddesses."

YOU'LL LAUGH, YOU'LL CRY

Comedy and tragedy, laughter and tears, are so intermixed; it's almost impossible to separate them from each other or from the human condition. This may well be the reason you see above many proscenium arches the intertwined masks of Pathos and Chaos, the traditional representations of Joy and Sorrow.

Comedy itself stems from slapstick (mastered by the Keystone Cops) and the crazies (the Marx Brothers, for example). It branches out into sophisticated humor (Cary Grant's bread and butter) and then into comedy teams (Laurel & Hardy, Olsen & Johnson, Abbott & Costello, Hope & Crosby, en Martin & Lewis). It buds into black humor (Dr. Strangelove) and more cently into the pseudo-neurosis of comics like Woody Allen. Comedy's roots ave produced many branches and a multitude of leaves and flowers.

> *In the language of screen comedians, four of the main grades of laugh are the titter, the yowl, the belly laugh, and the boffo.*
> — James Agee

> *Nobody should try to play comedy unless he has a circus going on inside.* — Ernst Lubitsch

> *Comedy is simply a funny way of being serious.* — Peter Ustinov

> *Comedy offers a more pessimistic world view than tragedy. Comedy deals, after all, with our limitations, not our freedom. It describes our trivial rather than our heroic concerns.* — Herman G. Weinberg

LAUREL &
HARDY

WOODY ALLEN

Woody Allen, born in 1935, started out as a gag writer, developed into a nightclub comedian, turned into a film writer, and blossomed as an actor-writer-director of such successful films as *Annie Hall* (1977), *Interiors* (1978), and *Manhattan* (1979). His specialty is neurotic Jewish guilt—New York style.

Not only is God dead, but try to get a plumber on weekends.

All literature is a footnote to Faust. *I have no idea what I mean by that.*

Most of the time I don't have much fun. The rest of the time I don't have any fun at all.

I failed to make the chess team, because of my height.

LAUREL & HARDY

To millions of kids around the world they were "Fat and Skin," Laurel and Hardy backwards. It was Oliver Hardy (1892-1957) who was fat. He was born in the United States and known affectionately as "Ollie." It was the English Stan Laurel (1890-1965) who was skinny, the writer of the scripts, and the producer of the films. They worked together from 1926 to 1940, starring in such pictures as *Babes in Toyland* (1934) and *A Chump at Oxford* (1940). Today their compilation films are the best known: *The Golden Age of Comedy* (1958), *When Comedy Was King* (1960), and *Days of Thrills and Laughter* (1961). Comedian Eddie Cantor said of them: "They play everything as if it might be *Macbeth* or *Hamlet.* That, to me, has always been a true sign of comic genius."

LAUREL:
All I know is just how to make people laugh.

I had a very beautiful sneer even if I say so myself.

HARDY:
We had fun, and we did a lot of crazy things in our pictures, but we were always real.

I know they're dumber than anyone else, but there are plenty of Laurels and Hardys in the world.

ABBOTT & COSTELLO

It's fashionable to downplay Abbott and Costello and dismiss them as "cross-talking vaudevillians" much inferior to Laurel & Hardy. But when they were good, they were very good indeed. They worked together from 1939 to 1956. Bud Abbott (1895-1974), the thin one, played both bully and straight man to Lou Costello (1906-1959), the dumpy one who seemed tongue-tied when he had to explain something to his exasperated buddy. Among their best movies are *Ride 'Em Cowboy* (1941), *The Naughty Nineties* (1945), and the "monster pictures" in which they meet the likes of Frankenstein, the Killer, Dr. Jekyll and Mr. Hyde, and the Mummy.

Here's the opening of their most memorable routine, from *The Naughty Nineties:*

BUD:

> Now, on the St. Louis team we have Who's on first, What's on second, I Don't Know is on third—

LOU:

> That's what I want to find out. I want you to tell me the names of the fellows on the St. Louis team.

BUD:

> I'm telling you. Who's on first, What's on second, I Don't Know is on third—

ABBOTT, following Lou Costello's death:

> I never understood Lou.

COSTELLO, dying words:

> That was the best ice-cream soda I ever tasted.

CLOSE-UPS

Together Bud and Lou were sublimely funny. — Mel Brooks

They flashed like twin meteors across a summer sky, dazzling the nation with their bright, brash, totally unsophisticated comedy.
— Bob Thomas

W.C. FIELDS

Mean, mendacious, larcenous, misanthropic, antisocial are some of the adjectives that describe the screen appearance (and, to some extent, the real personality) of W.C. Fields (1879-1946). A former vaudeville juggler, Fields continued to surprise audiences with his verbal acrobatics in such pictures as *You Can't Cheat an Honest Man* (1939), *My Little Chickadee* (1940), and *Never Give a Sucker an Even Break* (1941). He was superbly cast as Mr. Micawber in *David Copperfield* (1934). Many of his most characteristic, curmudgeonly lines come from the films he wrote himself.

> Any man who hates small dogs and children can't be all bad.

> Marriage is a two-way proposition, but never let the woman know she is one of the two ways.

> Women are like elephants to me: I like to look at them, but I wouldn't want to own one.

> There may be some things better than sex, and some things may be worse, but there is nothing exactly like it.

> I can lick my weight in wildflowers.

> I never met a kid I liked.

> Somebody put too many olives in my martini last night.

> Don't drink the water. Fish fuck in it.

> I got Mark Hellinger so drunk last night that it took three bellboys to put me to bed.

> I'm like Robin Hood—I take from the rich and give to the poor—us poor.

W.C.
FIELDS
1944

If at first you don't succeed, try, try again. Then quit. No use being a damn fool about it.

Never give a sucker an even break.

You can't cheat an honest man.

Hold your breath and lie down.

Drat!

BUSTER KEATON

The unsmiling features of Buster Keaton (1895-1966) have brought smiles to the faces of millions of fans from the Twenties to the Sixties. Such early slapstick comedies of the silent era as *The Navigator* (1924) and *The General* (1926) are as cherished as the deadpan comedian's appearances in *Sunset Boulevard* (1950) and *Limelight* (1952). A triumph of his later years is *The Railroader* (1965), in which he clowns his way across Canada by rail.

My ancestors didn't come on the Mayflower, but they met the boat.

People may talk it up or talk it down, but my face has been a valuable trademark for me during my sixty years in show business.

I never realized that I was doing anything but trying to make people laugh when I threw my custard pies and took my pratfalls.

Our hero came from NOWHERE. He wasn't going ANYWHERE and he got kicked out of SOMEWHERE.

Audiences love The Slow Thinker.

Fall, and the world laughs at you.

A comedian does funny things; a good comedian does things funny.

As long as the Tibetan peasants don't know how to spell your name, you are not a star.

CLOSE-UPS

Buster Keaton was in fact missed rather than forgotten. — British critic Dilys Powell writing of Keaton's period of eclipse after the rise of sound.

Buster Keaton's motto seems to be "Fall, and the world laughs at you." — Robert E. Sherwood

THE MARX BROTHERS

"Ruthless burlesque," "concentrated anarchy," "highly creative destructive-ness" are phrases used by critics to describe Marx Brothers' pictures like *Animal Crackers* (1930) and *A Night at the Opera* (1935). Groucho (1895-1977) the cigar-smoking wisecracker, was backed in acts of marvellous mayhem by his two brothers, Chico (1891-1961), an Italian-accented pianist, and Harpo (1893-1964), a mock-mute harpist. Two other Marx Brothers, Gummo (born 1897) and Zeppo (born 1901), were active in vaudeville productions but not in films. An *ex-officio* Marx Brother was the imposing dowager actress Margaret Dumont (1890-1965), the butt of many of their routines.

GROUCHO:
> *There are three things that my brother Chico is always on: a phone, a horse, or a broad.*

CHICO:
> *"??"*

HARPO:
> *I am the most fortunate self-taught harpist and non-speaking actor who ever lived.*

GUMMO:
> *Groucho's surgery is so minor that he even thought about doing it himself but couldn't find anyone to hold the mirror.*

ZEPPO:
> *Hey, how are you? How've you been? How's your family? I've never seen you before in by life.*

GROUCHO:
> *The contrary is also true.*

G. MARX

No one is completely unhappy at the failure of his best friend.

Please accept my resignation. I don't care to belong to any club that will have me as a member.

An amateur thinks it's funny if you dress a man up as an old lady, put him in a wheelchair, and give the wheelchair a push that sends it spinning down a slope toward a stone wall. For a pro it's got to be a real old lady.

A wife has a lot of nerve expecting her husband to be faithful when she gets old and fat.

Women have two rackets going for them—marriage and alimony.

There will be no trains sold until the magazines have left the station.

Karl Marx was not one of the Marx Brothers. He was one of the Ritz Brothers.

Anyone can get old. All you have to do is live long enough.

I hope they bury me near a straight man.

MARGARET DUMONT:

I was told that they needed an actress with dignity and poise, to lend legitimate balance to their comedy. After three weeks as Groucho's leading lady, I nearly had a nervous breakdown.

Cecilia Anger, the film writer, declared:

There ought to be a statue erected, or a Congressional Medal awarded, or a national holiday proclaimed, to honor that great woman, Margaret Dumont, the dame who takes the raps from the Marx Brothers.

CLOSE-UPS

Nobody could follow the Marx Brothers. It was impossible.
—Jack Benny

Imagine the Marx Brothers knowing me!— Zasu Pitts

Cedric Hardwicke is my fifth favorite actor, the first four being the Marx Brothers.— George Bernard Shaw

MICKEY MOUSE

The world's best-known rodent, the most-loved cartoon figure of all time, the most successful specimen of animation ever, has to be Mickey Mouse. The colorful comic figure was born in the Walt Disney studios in Hollywood in 1928 and was almost christened Mortimer Mouse. Ub Iwerks drew the appealing features, and Disney himself recorded the high-pitched mouse's voice in *Steamboat Willie* (1928). Perhaps his most memorable appearance on the screen was in *Fantasia* (1940), where he plays the Sorcerer's Apprentice.

CLOSE-UPS

I know one star in Hollywood who hasn't been spoiled by success, and that is Mickey Mouse.— Eddie Cantor

Newsreels and Mickey Mouse, these are the only pictures I like. — William Faulkner

The two great contributions of the screen to date are Mickey Mouse and Charlie Chaplin, one synthetic, the other select. — Raymond Massey

The President never has an evening of his own planning without at least one Mickey Mouse film. — Eleanor Roosevelt

I don't relate to Mickey as a rodent but as a comic character of the grand proportion. Along with the swastika and the Coca-Cola bottle, Mickey Mouse is the most powerful graphic image of the 20th Century. — Ernest Trova

Mickey Mouse hasn't lacked competition; we have also:

BUGS BUNNY:
  What's up, Doc?

About this hair-brained hare, the surrealist artist Salvador Dali said:

Bugs Bunny is the most ugly and frightening animal in the world. I will paint it with mayonnaise and make it an object of art.

DONALD DUCK:
  Quack, quack!

FRITZ THE CAT:
  We're not restricted for nothin', baby!

WOODY WOODPECKER
  Da-da-de-da-da, da-da-de-da-da!

PORKY PIG:
  Th-tha-that's all, folks!

A CLUSTER OF COMICS

GRACIE ALLEN:
  Oh sure, everybody's got talent nowadays. But can he wrap it up?

JACK BENNY:
  It's absolutely true. I don't want to tell you how much insurance I carry with Prudential, but all I can say is—when I go, they go.

  If it isn't a Stradivarius, I've been robbed of $110.00.

  My money or my life? Well. . . .

GEORGE BURNS:
  People think all I have to do is to stand up and tell a few jokes. Well, that's not as easy as it looks. Every year it gets to be more of an effort to stand up.

JACKIE GLEASON:

All through an actor's life, failure is snapping at his heels like a giant mongrel dog. But because conceit is an actor's courage, he refuses to recognize that dog as anything more than a puppy who really can't harm him.

BOB HOPE:

You do a movie, and you have to wait to find out if it's any good. But personal appearance tours, that's instant satisfaction.

BERT LAHR:

Hollywood is the only community in the world where the entire population is suffering from rumortism.

I think you laugh at a great comedian because you want to cry. Laughter is never too far from tears.

People can applaud for you but they can't laugh for you.

Comedy is sympathy.

HARRY LANGDON:

Comedy is the satire of tragedy.

The oddest thing about this whole funny business is that the public really wants to laugh, but it's the hardest thing to make them do it. They don't want to cry, yet they will cry at the slightest provocation.

JERRY LEWIS:

My wife has a very important proclamation which goes, "Jerry Lewis is not allowed in this house." And any time I drag him in, he's not welcome. It's taught me a lot about myself.

I appeal to children, who know I get paid for doing what they get slapped for. I flout dignity and authority, and there's nobody alive who doesn't want to do the same thing.

There are three things that are real to me. . . God, human folly, and laughter. Since the first two are beyond our comprehension, we must do what we can with the third.

HAROLD LLOYD:

I was one of the first comics you could believe in.

ZERO MOSTEL:

In France the word comedien *actually means both comedian and actor.*

OLE OLSEN, of Olsen & Johnson:

I said to the audience, "May you live as long as you want," and he would say, "And may you laugh as long as you live." I guess that was sort of our motto.

SNUB POLLARD, of the Keystone Kops:

You know, I guess I've been bathed in no less than ten tons of very wet cement. I figured up once I'd caught about fourteen thousand pies in my puss and had been hit by six hundred automobiles and two trains. Once I was even kicked by a giraffe.

HAL ROACH:

So long as children are born, there'll be the same basis of comedy. There's nothing old and there's nothing new so far as children are concerned.

WILL ROGERS:

If a loan is made for a moving picture, the president of the bank wants to write the story for you. The directors want to know who the leading lady is, and if they could, they would keep her as collateral.

I'm not a real movie star—I still got the same wife I started out with nearly twenty-eight years ago.

Shakespeare is the only author that can play to losing business for hundreds of years and still be known as an author.

There is only one thing that can kill the movies, and that is education.

MACK SENNETT, "king of comedy":

Any little success I have had was because I was one of the mob and catered to the mob.

I have my fingers on the public pulse. If I laugh at a gag on the screen, I know the public will laugh.

You know, the art of screen slapstick has been mostly lost. Yet people love slapstick. The lowering of dignity is always funny. There is a great deal of humor in the combination of surprise and violence.

We were awash with pretty women, clowns, and story-tellers who couldn't write. We made a million dollars so fast my fingers ached from trying to count.

Actress Dorothy Granger added:

I had heard from others that Mack Sennett was a real s.o.b. to actors when he directed them. But he was as nice as pie (custard, that is) to me.

JACQUES TATI:

What is demanded above all of a comic actor is a training in sport.

The possibility of opening a terrace on to life and making known all its riches seems to me one of the many uses of the cinema.

It is necessary for my characters to evolve, not for my camera to move.

I didn't invent Hulot. You can see him everywhere.

KEENAN WYNN, on a poor comedian:
When he laughed, dust came out of his mouth.

MUSICAL EXTRAVAGANZAS

With the talkies came the Musical. In fact, the first talking picture, *The Jazz Singer* (1927), was a musical of sorts, with Al Jolson singing "Mammy," etc. With the wave of a baton, there was music and dancing on the screen. Some outstanding musicals, one for each decade, bring back memories of fast movement, of show girls, of lilting lyrics, of dancers' feet: *The Wizard of Oz* (1939), *Ziegfeld Follies* (1945), *An American in Paris* (1950), *West Side Story* (1961), *Cabaret* (1972)....

FRED ASTAIRE & GINGER ROGERS

What an unbeatable pair, Fred and Ginger! To millions, for decades, they epitomize grace in motion.

Born in 1899, Fred Astaire appeared in movies either as dancer or actor from 1933 to 1974. He is most fondly remembered for the nine motion pictures that paired him off with Ginger Rogers, a singer and comedienne as well as a dancing star, who was born in 1911.

Their pictures together are: *Flying Down to Rio* (1933), *Roberta* (1935), *Top Hat* (1935), *Follow the Fleet* (1936), *Swing Time* (1936), *Shall We Dance?* (1937), *Carefree* (1938), *The Story of Vernon and Irene Castle* (1939) and, after a lapse of some years, *The Barkleys of Broadway* (1948).

ASTAIRE:
I don't understand what people see in me. I don't look like a movie star and I don't act like a movie star. I'm just an old So and So from Omaha.

I don't dig this brooding, analytic stuff. I just dance, and I just act.

Each dance ought to spring somehow out of character or situation, otherwise it is simply a vaudeville act.

It was the kind of flop that made even the audience look bad.

For a long time now, they've had me retiring. I just don't intend to. And if I do, I'll never tell anybody.

ROGERS:
I loved Fred so, and I mean that in the nicest, warmest way: I had such affection for him artistically. I think of that experience with Fred as a divine blessing. It blessed me, and I don't think blessings are one-sided.

I wouldn't change places with Susie Glutz who works in an office for anything.

A star is too tired to do anything but go home, and so to bed and to sleep.

I live for today, that's why people think I'm strange. I don't even have a psychiatrist.

The most important thing in anyone's life is to be giving something. The quality I can give is fun and joy and happiness. This is my gift. . . I would not like a talent to go to waste.

On the dance floor: never be nervous!

CLOSE-UPS

She gave him sex and he gave her class.— Katharine Hepburn

Fred Astaire can dance a very intricate routine, and he makes it look so simple and easy. It gives the audience a sense of self-identification and a feeling that they, too, can do it.— Hermes Pan

BING CROSBY

Bing Crosby (1904-1977) was lucky and combined two careers with seeming ease. The first was that of a crooner with the big bands, famous later for "White Christmas"; the second, was that of a light comedy actor, who endeared himself to millions with such movies as *Going My Way* (1944) and the famous "Road" movies with Bob Hope—seven of them—beginning with *The Road to Singapore* (1939). One of Crosby's most pleasant traits was that of seeming never to take himself too seriously.

My favorite kind of picture would be one that opened with a shot of me sitting in a rocking chair on a front porch. The rest of the picture would be what I saw.

Look, don't put too much stuff for me in these scenes. I do two kinds of acting—loud and soft.

Once or twice I've been described as a light comedian. I consider this the most accurate description of my abilities I've ever seen. That's just about all I am, a light comedian.

CLOSE-UP

Bing sings like all people think they sing in the shower.
— Dinah Shore

GENE KELLY

Those two words—Gene Kelly—were practically synonymous with the Hollywood musical in the 1940's and 50's. Actor, dancer, choreographer, Kelly was all of these. Among his outstanding pictures are: *For Me and My Gal* (1942), *An American in Paris* (1951), *Singin' in the Rain* (1952), *Brigadoon* (1954), and *Inherit the Wind* (1960). Kelly's style is strong and masculine.

The joy of my kind of dancing is that you never forget it's an eternal fertility rite.

A choreographer takes an idea out of his head and transposes it on people's anatomy.

My style is strong, wide-open bravura. Fred's is intimate, cool, easy. 95

CLOSE-UPS

My respect for him as a person and as an artist is unbounded.
— Fred Astaire

If they ever get around to handing out Oscars for outstanding performance as a human being, you'll know where to find Ol' Blue Eyes—on the nominating committee rooting for his old buddy, Gene. — Frank Sinatra

FRANK SINATRA

"Ol' Blue Eyes", born in 1915, has held audiences since the 1940's with his talents as singer, actor, producer, concert and recording artist. His career has suffered ups and downs, but it has always been his own: highly individual. Among his notable movies are *Higher and Higher* (1943), *From Here to Eternity* (1953), *Guys and Dolls* (1956), and *The Detective* (1968).

When you are young, there is always someone around to spit on your dreams.

If I had as many love affairs as you fellows have given me credit for, I would now be speaking to you from inside a jar at the Harvard Medical School.

I'm for anything that gets you through the night, be it prayer, tranquilizers, or a bottle of Jack Daniels.

To reporters:
Is this going to take long?

Excuse me while I disappear.

CLOSE-UP

When Frank Sinatra was down he was sweet but when he got back up he was hell. — Ava Gardner

A MUSICAL MEDLEY

BUSBY BERKELEY:
I've made over one hundred movies, and before that staged dozens of Broadway musicals, and I never heard anyone calling them "camp"!

AARON COPLAND:
A well-placed dissonant chord can stop an audience cold in the middle of a sentimental scene, or a calculated woodwind passage can turn what appears to be a solemn moment into a belly-laugh.

HEDDA HOPPER:
Her singing was mutiny on the High C's.

1944

SINATRA — G. KELLY

LILLIAN GISH:
>The movies should have married music instead of words.

RUBY KEELER:
>It's amazing. I couldn't act. I had that terrible singing voice, and now I can see I wasn't the greatest tap dancer in the world either.

GYPSY ROSE LEE:
>Soon the actors will be all nude, the audience will be all nude, everyone will be nude except the police.
>
>I have everything now I had twenty years ago—except it's all lower.

WLADZIU VALENTINO LIBERACE:
>Remember that bank I used to cry all the way to? I bought it.

JEANETTE MACDONALD:
>If I ever publish my memoirs they will be called **The Iron Butterfly.**

MARY MARTIN:
>I beat my brains out, and I like to hear the echo.

ANN MILLER:
>I've danced with my toe nails broken and bleeding, with swollen feet, with blood clots in my leg. Not all at the same time, of course. But I always managed to screw my earrings on tight.

SALLY RAND:
>The Rand is quicker than the eye.

JACK ROSE:
>Lyrics heard on this show were by Percy Bysshe Shelley, Alfred Lord Tennyson, Robert Browning—and Sammy Cahn.

MAX STEINER:
>It's a great fallacy to think that a bad picture can be saved by good music. It may be helped a little bit, but that's all. Similarly, a good picture can't be ruined by the worst possible music. But sometimes I wonder.

EVA TANGUAY:
>I don't care...I really don't.

DIMITRI TIOMKIN, accepting an Oscar:
>Thank you. I did it all by myself.
>
>On another occasion:
>How do you score an orgasm?

SOPHIE TUCKER:
>I have been poor, and I have been rich. Rich is better.

RUDY VALLEE:
>I'm a product of radio—that powerful medium, which at one time was a great part of our lives but since has become, like silent movies, a voice lost in the wilderness.

HORSE OPERAS

"Stick 'em up!" "They went that-a-way." "When you say that, smile." "Meanwhile, back at the ranch...."

The Western, as a form, is almost as old as the movies themselves. *The Great Train Robbery,* made in 1903, and eleven minutes in length, was a Western. Here's one for each decade since: *The Squaw Man* (1913), *The Virginian* (1929), *Stagecoach* (1939), *Red River* (1949), *Shane* (1953), *Butch Cassidy and the Sundance Kid* (1969), and *Yuma* (1970).

The stern morality, the sense of movement and excitement, the feeling for the wide open spaces and the great outdoors, and the clear distinction between "good guys" and "bad guys," whether they be white men or Indians, farmers or ranchers, settlers or rustlers, are reasons for the continued popularity of the cowboy movie.

The march to the West is our Odyssey.— André Bazin

There will always be an audience for the Western, for the Western represents romantic adventure and idealism, achievement, optimism for the future, justice, individualism, the beauty of the land, and the courage and independence of the individuals who won the land.
— William K. Everson

During these years it was only the lowly Western, made outdoors in natural surroundings by force of restricted budgets as well as story necessity, that kept alive a tradition of using real backgrounds and props and some simple, natural incidents.— Ernest Callenbach

I keep wishing I could sneak off and do a couple of quickie Westerns, just to make sure I still know how.— Frank Capra

I'd like to have been a Western star. An actor feels more like a man when he has spurs on his boots and is riding across the prairie, the wind leathering his face.— Clark Gable

Any story can be transformed to a Western simply by providing the background.— Andrew McLaglen

A cowboy actor needs only two changes of expression—hat on and hat off.— Fred MacMurray

MEN ON HORSEBACK

GENE AUTRY, "singing cowboy":
I'm back in the saddle again....

After three decades of riding into the sunset, Gene Autry now owns it.— Pat Buttram

GILBERT M. ANDERSON, known as Broncho Billy:
And as for marksmanship, heck, in those movies a blank used to turn a corner and kill a man.

WILLIAM BOYD, who played Hopalong Cassidy:
I'm not the man people remember as Hopalong Cassidy. They'd be shocked at the difference.

GARY COOPER:

I want, before my life is over, to go back to Montana.

An oil man is allowed to deplete twenty-seven per cent annually as the oil is used up. An industrialist can depreciate his equipment as it ages. Now all I have to sell is me—this body of mine. If it's maimed or broken, I can't work. And it ages just as certainly as machine tools. But do they let me depreciate it? Heck, no.

WILLIAM S. HART:

The truth of the West meant more to me than a job, and always will.

I don't know how much the Western film means to Europe; but to this country it means the very essence of national life.

These hills were mine and had been mine since my birth.

BUCK JONES:

So good luck, and Vaya Con Dios, as the vaqueros say.

KEN MAYNARD:

Not all heroes die on the battlefields.

TOM MIX:

If God was good enough to give me a full head of hair, the least I can do is keep it dyed.

Always find time for a good deed.

Straight shooters always win!

ROY ROGERS:

I'm goin' to stand up for America until somebody shoots me.

When you're young and you fall off a horse you may break something. When you're my age and you fall off, you splatter.

I told Dale, "When I go, just skin me and put me on top of Trigger."

JOHN WAYNE:

Life, death, courage, good and evil. No nuances. Give'em a little scenery, a little action. And then, if you've got a good personal story and good characterization, you've got a film with universal appeal.

SHIVERS AND SHRIEKS

We call them all "horror pictures" but they really divide into "films of horror" and "films of terror." The distinction is between horrors which endanger our bodies and terrors which threaten our souls. Thus, Dr. Frankenstein's Monster will maim or murder us, but Count Dracula will curse or damn us for all eternity. Whether physical or psychological, monsters, menaces, and things that "go bump" in the night are a staple of screen entertainment. Something is buried deep within the human psyche that requires a confrontation with prehistoric creatures, monsters from the depths of space, or demons from the far and dark reaches of the soul.

Let's listen now to some of the "monsters" and monster-makers. Actually, you'll probably find them a likeable bunch: Bradbury is almost lyrical on his art, and Karloff comes across as a gentle soul; Lugosi, though, will provoke some with his observation on the true audience for horror movies.

RAY BRADBURY:

Tonight the Prince of Darkness walks among you. We hold him high, shake his bones. We fan his wings, expose his teeth. His shadow quakes your seat. Is he not magnificent, is he not beautiful? Shiver sweet agonies from this encounter.

WILLIAM CASTLE:

I suppose you could say I've devoted my career to scaring the hell out of people.

We all have a common interest, bigger and more horrible monsters—and I'm just the monster to bring them to you.

I say an audience doesn't know what they want to see, but they know what they don't want to see.

LON CHANEY, "man of a thousand faces":

I hope I shall never be accused of striving merely for horrible effects.

I've never worn a mask in my life, save at Halloween parties.

LON CHANEY, JR.:

I positively will not cash in on the fame which my Dad earned by his years of hard work and suffering in the grotesque roles he played.

The make-up is merely the beginning.

The Wolf Man didn't want to do all those things—he was forced into them.

Find something no one else can do, and they'll begin to take notice of you.

ROGER CORMAN, "King of the B's":

Some of the most frightening sequences I've ever shot are simply a camera dollying up to a strange door and hearing some strange noise—not necessarily a violent noise.

PETER CUSHING:

Who wants to see me do Hamlet? Very few. But millions want to see me as Frankenstein, so that's the one I do.

BORIS KARLOFF:

It is not true that I was born a monster. Hollywood made me one.

Suddenly, out of the eerie darkness and gloom, there swept on the screen, about eight times larger than life itself, the chilling horrendous figure of me as the Monster!

LON CHANEY JR.
LUGOSI
KARLOFF

My dear old monster, I owe everything to him. He's my best friend.

CHRISTOPHER LEE:

If someone were to take a survey of cinema audiences and the kind of pictures they like, I have a feeling the horror film would come out as number one in popularity.

What I try to do is to give the audience a sense of anxiety, to make it worry. An audience should ask, "What's he going to do next?" This is the essence of suspense.

Ours is a business both strange and unique, a business of starlight and glamor—one moment a place of dreams, the next of nightmares.

BELA LUGOSI:

How can any man be sad and watch a sunset?

The screen magnifies everything, even the way you are thinking.

Although I'm afraid I'm typed by now, I'd like to quit the supernatural roles every third time and play just an interesting, down-to-earth person. One of these days I may get my wish! Meanwhile, I'll take any story if it's good.

It is women who love horror. Gloat over it. Feed on it. Are nourished by it. Shudder and cling and cry out—and come back for more. Women have a predestination to suffering.

If I had one per cent of the millions Dracula has made, I wouldn't be sitting here now.

JAMES H. NICHOLSON, film executive:

Each time our monster got his deserts, we had actually enacted a modern version of the medieval morality play. We had filmed Everyman.

VINCENT PRICE:

Nobody would be in this business if he were normal.

It's hard to make the unbelievable believable, and that's what we have to do. It's also hard not to break up while you're doing it.

They'll have to bury me before I retire, and even then my tombstone will read: "I'll be back!"

SLAVKO VORKAPICH, cinematographer:

Fear is something behind you.

LOVE GODDESSES

It seems incredible today, given the suggestiveness of movies produced during the silent era, and the permissiveness of those released in the Sixties and Seventies, that such words as "mistress" and "seduction" and "virgin" were not permitted in films, and that the first time they *were* heard was on the soundtrack of *The Moon Is Blue* (1953), a harmless bit of froth directed by Otto Preminger and released without the approval of the Production Code or the Legion of Decency.

We are all voyeurs in the dark, hoping, desirous of a glimpse, no matter how fleeting, of the forbidden, the illicit, the explicit. Jean Harlow was raunchy, Brigitte Bardot innocent and kittenish, Marilyn Monroe open and vulnerable. Mae West ridiculed it all, and the Gabors travestied the very notion of sexuality. They are all (by my books) Love Goddesses, some tarnished, some fallen, some desirable, some as ugly as many idols are.

There are no really comparable Love Gods here. A chapter of social commentary would be required to explain this phenomenon.

BRIGITTE BARDOT

Do the initial letters "B.B." stand for "BaBy" or "Blonde Bombshell" or Brigitte Bardot. During the Fifties and Sixties, in the public mind, they stood for Brigitte Bardot, the French "sex kitten" who was born in 1935. She was brought to world attention by Roger Vadim who enterprisingly displayed her voluptuous body to a great advantage in *And God Created Woman* (1956). She appeared in a succession of films and became an actress of sorts, but one whose name and initials are synonymous with a kind of freeflowing sexuality and uninhibited lifestyle.

> *Time will destroy me one day, as it destroys everything. But no one else will ever be Bardot. I am the only Bardot, and my species is unique.*

> *I am not an actress. I am a phenomenon.*

> *I cannot play roles. I can only play me—on and off the screen.*

> *I play myself. I'm not good enough to play somebody else.*

> *That's why I like simple, wild, sexy parts.*

> *I have absolutely no ambition. I just want to live, and be happy.*

> *There is a French proverb: To live happy, live hidden. Where can Brigitte Bardot hide?*

> *When I am alone, I am lost.*

> *I leave before being left. I decide.*

> *Love is the most important thing in my life. Without it, I cannot survive. After love, way, way down, comes everything else.*

> *For me, love needs mystery, secrecy and silence.*

> *Most of the nice things that happen to me seem to happen overnight.*

> *A woman is a tender and sweet person. She'll lose that if she tries to be like a man.*

> *If you live with a man, you must conquer him every day. Otherwise, he will go to another.*

Sometimes I feel like the only woman in the world.

A good actress lasts, and sex attraction does not.

You must at least be amusing, the best at something, or interesting, otherwise you will be nothing!

Being famous imprisons you.

Was it me that Botticelli imagined?

Photographers have ruined my life.

I've been condemned from more pulpits than Satan.

If people don't like me, I become very plain.

For me, art annihilates life.

THE GABORS

Some see the Gabors as great fun; others see them as the triumph of tastelessness. The Hungarian-born mother and two daughters, whether consciously or not, burlesque sex and security-counsciousness for all they're worth. Jolie is the mother of Eva (born 1921), who appeared in *Captain Kidd and the Slave Girl* (1954) and wrote an autobiography called *Orchids and Salami* (1954), and of Zsa Zsa (born 1919), who appeared in *Moulin Rouge* (1953), *Queen of Outer Space* (1959), and *Arrivederci Baby* (1966).

JOLIE:

It's just as easy to fall in love with a rich man as with a poor man.

Before he died, leaving behind half a million dollars, poor vunderfool George Sanders realized that to be glamorous means to be Gaborised.

There are no wrinkles on the heart.

ZSA ZSA:

If I've shocked you, darlings, I'm glad.

Oh, what a pretty dress—and so cheap!

Let's talk about hippies. Did you know I am the first elegant hippie?

Sure, dollink. Come back and see me after my next marriage.

Conrad Hilton and I had one thing in common. We both wanted his money.

We were both in love with George Sanders.

George loves me dearly. He'd better—a fourth divorce would ruin him.

I never hated a man enough to give him back his diamonds. Money? It's expendable.

Husbands are like fires. They go out when unattended.

Who but a voyeur wants to watch somebody else make love?

A girl must marry for love, and keep on marrying until she finds it.

Every man in this world needs a Zsa Zsa.

CLOSE-UPS

I lived in Zsa Zsa's sumptuous Bel Air mansion as a sort of paying guest. — George Sanders

Marriage is for bores. I mean Gabors. — Oscar Levant

JEAN HARLOW

The phrase "platinum blonde" best describes Jean Harlow (1911-37) who specialized in playing the slattern on the screen. She brought to her roles a salty characterization that went over well in the Thirties and which retains its charm almost half a century later. She appeared in Chaplin's *City Lights* (1931) as an extra. Harlow's principal films are *Platinum Blonde* (1931), *Red-Headed Woman* (1932), and, with Clark Gable, *Red Dust* (1932).

If audiences like you, you don't have to be an actress.

The men like me because I don't wear a brassiere. And the women like me because I don't look like a girl who would steal a husband. At least not for long.

The public—even the ones who don't like me—are my friends.

Any romance? Sure! The one I'm having with the world.

No man has ever loved me before for what's best in me.

I like to wake up feeling a new man.

That's one of the troubles with American women. They're always going to bed, but for the wrong reasons.

I have to live up to my publicity.

I wore a low-cut gown, and overnight I became a hussy.

What kind of whore am I now? [*To a producer*]

Greta Garbo and Carole Lombard and Norma Shearer seem like real movie stars to me. But I have always felt more like an outsider who got an unbelievable break in Hollywood.

CLOSE-UP

Tell me, how does a girl like Harlow, a temple of sex, wind up married to a fairy bigamist? Tell me! — Louis B. Mayer on Harlow's disastrous marriage to film executive Paul Bern.

MARILYN MONROE

Marilyn Monroe (1926-62) was the last of the great sex symbols . . . so far, at least. But this should not obscure her talent for light comedy. She played to perfection Lorelei Lee in *Gentlemen Prefer Blondes* (1953) and Sugar in *Some Like It Hot* (1959). But, surrounding this voluptuous beauty, there was always the suggestion of tragedy. At the time of her death she had been working on *Something's Got to Give*, which remains incomplete.

Monroe: a complex woman, who won't be pigeon-holed and who meant many different things to many different people.

I was one of a family of many children, and Clark Gable was our father, and he liked me the best. Each night, when he came home, he'd swing me up onto his shoulder and tell me how pretty I was. Of all the children, he loved me the best.

I knew I belonged to the public and to the world, not because I was talented or even beautiful but because I had never belonged to anyone else. The public was the only family, the only Prince Charming, and the only home I had ever dreamed about.

I have too many fantasies to be a housewife.

It's nice to be included in people's fantasies, but you also like to be accepted for your own sake.

If you look hard at people, you find they look so unhappy.

Five minutes after I'm there, they'll forget I was late.

It's not really me that's late; it's the others who are always in a hurry.

Your big enemy is loneliness.

Sometimes I know the truth of what I'm doing.

I've always felt those articles somehow reveal more about the writers than they do about me.

I can't memorize the words by themselves. I have to memorize the feelings.

First, I'm trying to prove to myself that I'm a person. Then maybe I'll convince myself that I'm an actress.

A career is born in public—talent in privacy.

An actress is not a machine, but they treat you like one. A money machine.

Only the public can make a star. It's the studios who try and make a system out of it.

I don't want to make money, I just want to be wonderful. I'll be smart—tomorrow.

Hollywood's a place where they'll pay you a thousand dollars for a kiss, and fifty cents for your soul.

Fame is a special burden.

You might as well try to make yourself fly as to make yourself love.

People say I walk all wiggly and wobbly. I don't know what they mean. I just walk.

I never understood it—the sex symbol—I always thought symbols were things you clash together. That's the trouble, a sex symbol becomes a thing—I just hate to be a thing. But if I'm going to be a symbol of something, I'd rather have it sex.

Sex is important to me. I think one of the reasons why everyone thinks me so sexy is that I think sex all the time. I wonder about sex with every man I meet, and they sense it and—well, respond.

Sex is part of nature, and I go along with nature.

When I'm in love I feel good—sometimes all over.

I still love everybody a little that I ever loved.

What did I put on for sleeping? Chanel No. 5.

I like to feel blonde all over.

Television sets should be taken out of bedrooms.

The trouble with the censor is that he worries if a girl has cleavage. He should worry if she hasn't any.

On the phone to actor Peter Lawford the night of her suicide:

Say goodbye to Pat, say goodbye to the President, and say goodbye to yourself because you're a nice guy.

CLOSE-UPS

Marilyn was born the postwar day we had need of her. Certainly she had no knowledge of the past. Like Giraudoux's Ondine, she is only fifteen years old; and she will never die.— Cecil Beaton

There's a broad with a future behind her.— Constance Bennett

There's something extremely alert and vivid in her, an intelligence. It's her personality, it's a glance, it's something very tenuous, very vivid that disappears quickly, that appears again.— Henri Cartier-Bresson

Strictly speaking, she wasn't beautiful, but she came alive on the screen. She was born to appear on the screen—a very talented person who never trusted her own talent.— George Cukor

Necking with Marilyn Monroe is like kissing Hitler.— Tony Curtis

I want those roses put there three times a week—forever.

If it wasn't for some of her friends, she wouldn't be where she is.
— Joe DiMaggio, husband

Say a prayer for Norma Jean. She's dead.
— First husband, Jim Dougherty

My interest in Marilyn's career was not for gain. She needed me at the time, and I put at her complete disposal whatever abilities I possessed. — Milton Greene

It's Jean Harlow all over again. — Ben Lyon

Marilyn made me lose all sympathy for actresses. In most of her takes, she was either fluffing lines or freezing. She didn't bother to learn her lines. I don't hink she could act her way out of a paper script. She has no charm, delicacy or taste. She's just an arrogant little tail-twitcher who's learned to throw sex in your face. — Nunnally Johnson

You are a very lovely young lady. — Nikita Khruschchev

Mr. President, this lovely lady... this one lovely lady who has done so much... who has meant so much... here she is, Mr. President... the late Marilyn Monroe.... — Peter Lawford, introducing the star at President John F. Kennedy's birthday party

Now I can retire from politics after having had "Happy Birthday" sung to me by such a sweet, wholesome girl as Marilyn Monroe.
— John F. Kennedy

She was our angel, the sweet angel of sex, and the sugar of sex came up from her like the resonance of sound in the clearest grain of a violin... a very Stradivarius of sex. — Norman Mailer

Marilyn Monroe? A vacuum with nipples. — Otto Preminger

Billy Wilder once said, "Marilyn Monroe is a mean seven-year-old girl." I think he missed it by about a year and a half. — Billy Wilder as quoted by Tony Curtis

Anyone who could make her smile came as a blessing to me. With a little luck, she might have made it.

I think she was trying to go back to her girlhood, and yet she couldn't. She was trying to surround herself with gaiety, but it wasn't working. — Arthur Miller, husband

MAE WEST

Even the titles of Mae West's movies are titillating. The former vaudevillian, born in 1892, specialized in the satirization of sex and middle-class mores, with amusingly vulgar suggestiveness. *She Done Him Wrong* (1933) and *I'm No Angel* (1933) are two of her funniest films, mildly salacious at the time, witty and amusing today. She appeared with W.C. Fields in *My Little Chickadee* (1939), and made an amazing comeback in *Myra Breckinridge* (1970). Like her movies, her autobiography has a good title: *Goodness Had Nothing To Do With It* (1959).

Sex is an emotion in motion.

Love conquers all things except poverty and toothache.

I used to be Snow White, but I drifted.

When I'm good, I'm very good. When I'm bad, I'm better.

It's not the men in my life that counts—it's the life in my men.

I'm a fast-movin' girl that likes 'em slow.

Every man I meet wants to protect me. Can't figure out from whom.

When they make a man better than George Raft, I'll make him too.

It takes two to make trouble for one.

A man has more character in his face at thirty than twenty—he's suffered longer.

I'm proud to be eighty-two because I know I don't look it.

I'm the only antique in the movie industry—and you know how much antiques cost.

I'm happy I don't wake up to find my name in the obituary column.

Come up and see me sometime.

Beulah, peel me a grape.

Goodness had nothing to do with it, honey.

Kiss me, my fool.

Thanks, I enjoyed every inch of it.

CLOSE-UPS

Only Charlie Chaplin and Mae West...dare to directly attack, with their mockery, the fraying morals and manners of a dreary world.— Hugh Walpole

In this picture, Mae West stole everything but the cameras.
— George Raft

I think I would rather let my daughters see Mae West's films regularly than see Hearst newspapers regularly....— Don Herold

6

The Producers

Without the producer, there would be no film.

No property would be acquired, no director hired, no technicians retained, no actors under contract. Without his efforts, no shorts or feature films would ever be exhibited in the moviehouses around the world. The producer puts the package together.

The producer may be an independent, nursing along a single feature, or an executive with a big studio, watching over dozens of feature films a year. Little or big, the producer is probably the most fascinating person in the film world, for he has to stand his ground in the crossfire between the backers of the film and the creative talents who put it together.

Seven producers are singled out here for special treatment. Two more are given their due elsewhere (Cecil B. DeMille among the directors, Samuel Goldwyn in a chapter all his own). These men—there's not a woman among them—and many more besides, have left their special marks on the screens of the world.

A short prologue:

I call myself an observer and a son-of-a-bitch; if you combine the two, you come very close to the qualitites of the ideal producer!
—Dmitri Tiomkin

I am convinced that movie audiences today are far ahead of the people who produce the pictures.— Eilia Kazan

They know only one word of more than one syllable here, and that is fillum.— Louis Sherwin

Whipped cream is good and herring is good, so they think they should be better together.— Curt Siodmak

Anyone permitted to tamper with the script will certainly do so, including the gaffer and the producer's wife.— Michael Wilson

I wish those sons of bitches like Louis B. Mayer and Harry Cohn were back with us because they loved films and made them.
— Shelley Winters

SELZNICK
ZANUCK
DISNEY

HARRY COHN

Next to Louis B. Mayer, Harry Cohn (1891-1958) had the dubious distinction of being the most despised producer in Hollywood, but he was as shrewd as he was crude. He helped form Columbia Pictures in 1924 and acted as its head of production from 1932 until his death. Among the pictures he produced were *All the King's Men* (1949) and *From Here to Eternity* (1953). He is satirized as the junk tycoon in Judy Holliday's *Born Yesterday* (1951).

It's not a business. It's a racket!

I am the king here. Whoever eats my bread, sings my song.

I don't have ulcers; I give them!

I have one rule. When a picture is great, they can take all the credit for it. When it stinks, I take the credit.

Seventy-five per cent of the ideas that people try to sell me are no good. If I turn down every idea at the outset, that makes me right seventy-five per cent of the time. That's not a bad average.

I have never met a grateful performer in the picture business.

Around this studio, the only Jews we put into pictures play Indians.

If you print anything good about me, nobody will believe it anyway.

Talent is only as good as the picture.

She's got talent and personality. Give me two years, and I'll make her an overnight star.

If you want to send a message, use Western Union.

I always know when there's something wrong with the story—my butt begins to itch.

CLOSE-UPS

Imagine—the whole world wired to Harry Cohn's ass!
— Herman J. Mankiewicz

I wish to be cremated when I die and my ashes to be thrown in Harry Cohn's face.— Norman Krasna

WALT DISNEY

Walt Disney (1901-1966) took animation to new heights and created a vast entertainment empire which not only produced motion-picture entertainment for the whole family but also spawned such playgrounds as Disneyland in California in 1955, and Walt Disney World in Florida in 1971. Disney created Mickey Mouse in 1928, Donald Duck in 1936, and True-Life Adventures (candid, nature short features) in 1948. His animated features, regularly re-released, include: *Pinocchio* (1939), *Fantasia* (1940), *Dumbo* (1941), *Bambi* (1942), *The Three Caballeros* (1944), *Cinderella* (1950), *Alice in Wonderland* (1951), and *Peter Pan* (1953). Disney's most successful live-action feature is *Mary Poppins* (1964).

I count my blessings.

I've never called my work art—it's show business.

I've always had a nightmare. I dream that one of my pictures has ended up in an art theater. And I wake up shaking.

I don't make films exclusively for children. I make them to suit myself, hoping they will also suit the audience.

All we are trying to do is give the public good entertainment. That is all they want.

All you've got to do is own up to your ignorance honestly, and you'll find people who are eager to fill your head with information.

When we do fantasy, we must not lose sight of reality.

Disneyland will never be completed, as long as there is imagination left in the world.

Laughter is a frown turned upside down!

There's enough ugliness and cynicism in the world without me adding to it.

I don't have any depressed moods, and I don't want to have any. I'm happy, just very, very happy

Walt's characteristic goodbye to kids:

May the Big Bad Wolf never come to your door.

CLOSE-UPS

Walt has always operated on the theory of making today pay off tomorrow. — Walt's brother, Roy O. Disney

I'm all for making Walt Disney our next Mayor. — Ray Bradbury

LOUIS B. MAYER

Louis B. Mayer (1885-1957) was one of the two most-hated producers in Hollywood. (The other was Harry Cohn of Columbia Pictures.) With the formation of Metro-Goldwyn-Mayer in 1924, he emerged as chief and held sway until 1951, when he was forced into retirement. His head of production was Irving Thalberg, and together they saw to it that MGM produced the most lavish pictures and maintained the most popular stable of talent.

I will go down on my knees to talent.

Some day you may even be as great as I am.

Why don't you sit on my lap when we're discussing your contract—the way the other girls do?

A woman's ass is for her husband, not theatergoers.

The number one book of the ages was written by a committee, and it was called the Bible.

When a producer tells me he has a prestige picture, I know we're going to lose money.

Look out for yourself or they'll pee on your grave.

CLOSE-UPS

Louis B. Mayer, not Louis the Eighteenth, was the last of the Bourbons.— Tom Buckley

Louis B. Mayer may be called Huckleberry Capone.

Louis B. Mayer admires with his whole soul the drivel his underlings produce in his factory.— Ben Hecht

Mayer is one of the real pioneers of Hollywood. He's done more for movies than dark balconies.

Louis B. Mayer came west in the early days with twenty-eight dollars, a box camera, and an old lion. He built a monument to himself—the Bank of America.— Bob Hope

There but for the grace of God, goes God.— Herman Mankiewicz

Put my ashes in a box, and tell the messenger to bring them to Louis B. Mayer's office with a farewell message from me. Then when the messenger gets to Louis' desk, I want him to open the box and blow the ashes in the bastard's face.— B.P. Schulberg

Two remarks are associated with Mayer's funeral. The first is sometimes attributed to Sam Goldwyn, the director:

The reason so many people showed up at Louis B. Mayer's funeral was because they wanted to make sure he was dead.

The second comes from comedian Red Skelton:

Well, it only proves what they always say—give the public something they want to see, and they'll come out for it.

CLOSE-UPS OF MGM

Every MGM picture is a good one. Some pictures are better than others, but there are no really bad pictures—at any rate there are no bad MGM pictures.— Louis B. Mayer

More Stars Than There Are In Heaven.— Howard Dietz

The MGM Lion no longer roars. On a quiet day, if you listen hard, you might hear Leo emit a mouse-like squeak as Jim Aubrey twists the poor, forlorn beast's tail. — Arthur H. Lewis

The only star at MGM is Leo the Lion. — Eddie Mannix

My Metro years were the best. I'd like to have them all back again. Favorite pictures? Any of the ones with Greer Garson.

I was like a kept woman during my twenty-one years at MGM. It was like an expensive, beautifully run club. You didn't need to carry money. Your face was your credit card—all over the world.
— Walter Pidgeon

When you worked for MGM, you worked for the best! It sure was fun while it lasted. — Pete Smith

All those years at Metro. . . I hid a black terror behind a cheerful face. — Robert Young

IRVING THALBERG

Irving Thalberg (1899-1936) entered the picture business early and died young, leaving a legend of youthful promise intact. As Louis B. Mayer's head of production, he saw to it that MGM produced a quality product that was much talked about. He produced pictures as dissimilar as *Grand Hotel* (1933) and *The Good Earth* (1937). Together with the lovely actress Norma Shearer, they reigned as "Hollywood's leading couple." F. Scott Fitzgerald captured Thalberg in the character of Monroe Stahr in his novel *The Last Tycoon*, filmed in 1976 with Robert De Niro playing the lead.

Always remember, there's nothing too good for the audience.

The medium will eventually take its place as art because there is no other medium of interest to so many people.

In short, it is a creative business, dependent, as almost no other business is, on the emotional reaction of its customers.

You've got a smash hit. A few more like that and you'll smash the industry.

To hell with art this time. I'm going to produce a picture that will make money.

Nobody has been able to say definitely whether picture-making is really a business or an art. Personally I think it is both.

I believe that although the motion picture will not live forever as a work of art, except in a few instances, it will be the most effective way of showing posterity how we live now.

What's all this business about being a writer? It's just putting one word after another.

If you have the power to put your name on the screen, your name on the screen is meaningless.

If you are in a position to give credit yourself, then you do not need it.

I don't think this picture could survive a lot of improvement.

To his wife Norma Shearer, on his deathbed in Hollywood:

Don't let the children forget me.

CLOSE-UPS

Irving Thalberg saved me from the breadline. — John Barrymore

How can I compete with Norma Shearer, when she sleeps with the boss? — Joan Crawford

On the way down, I saw Thalberg's shoes in the hall, and no one has filled them. — Gene Fowler

On a clear day you can see Thalberg.

Mr. Thalberg, do you want it [the script] *Wednesday or good?*
— George S. Kaufman

Irving Thalberg carried with him the accoutrements of an artist; hence he was unique in the Hollywood of the period. I don't know of anyone else who has occupied that position. He was like a young pope.
— Budd Schulberg

To Thalberg all life is a soda fountain. . . . Thalberg is the epic of the common man. — Jim Tully

DAVID O. SELZNICK

David O. Selznick (1902-1965) was born into a film family. His father, Lewis, was a pioneer producer; his brother, Myron, became a leading agent, and he himself was once Louis B. Mayer's son-in-law. He formed Selznick International in 1936 and personally produced the blockbuster *Gone With the Wind* (1939). Other Selznick productions include *Rebecca* (1940), *Duel in the Sun* (1946), and *A Farewell to Arms* (1957). He took an active interest in the career of his wife, actress Jennifer Jones.

I always worked on the theory that if you make your picture one per cent better you might improve your take ten per cent.

There are only two classes—first class and no class.

Once in a blue moon, a picture comes along that makes one proud to be in the picture business. . . .

Vivien Leigh, whose father is French and mother Irish, will play the role of Scarlett O'Hara, whose father was Irish and mother French.

I've got to do better than Gone With the Wind. *I may never make it. But I've got to try.*

Once photographed, life here is ended. It is almost symbolic of Hollywood. Tara had no rooms inside. It was just a facade. When I go they'll put on my tombstone, "Here lies the man who made Gone With the Wind.*"*

CLOSE-UPS

Yes, it has been wonderful, but I don't think it has been worth it.
— Irene Mayer Selznick, wife

I hate all producers—except my brother. And I even hate him, when he's acting like a producer.

I'll break them all! I'll send all those thieves and fourflushers crawling to the poorhouse. Before I'm done, the artists in this town will have all the money.

Stars should get the money while they can. Their careers don't last very long. — Myron Selznick, brother

David took after his father, Lewis J. Selznick, the film pioneer, who sent the following telegram to the Czar of Russia, when he learned of the Russian Revolution:

When I was a boy in Russia your police treated my people very badly. However no hard feelings. Hear you are now out of work. If you will come to New York, can give you fine position acting in pictures. Salary no object. Reply my expense. Regards you and family.

It was Lewis who said:

My stars don't ride on streetcars.

I pledge myself to make clean pictures just as naturally as I would pledge myself not to drink prussic acid, leap into a blast furnace, or throw myself in front of a railroad train.

Spend it all. Give it away. But get rid of it. Live expensively. If you have confidence in yourself, live beyond your means. Then you'll have to work hard to catch up. That's the only fun there is: hard work. Never try to save money. If you do, then you have two things to worry about: Making it, and keeping it. Just concern yourself with making it. The rest will take care of itself.

JACK L. WARNER

With his three brothers Harry, Albert and Sam, Jack L. Warner, born in 1892, established Warner Brothers, a major studio, in 1919. A hard-hitting businessman with an instinct for what the public wants, Warner himself kept a hand in production. His films go from the first talkie, *The Jazz Singer* (1927), to *My Fair Lady* (1964).

I have created enough stars, if I may use the word "create" modestly, to fill the Hollywood skies.

I believe—and box-office returns will confirm it—that the most profitable pictures are those made by men who understand every nerve and muscle and vein that make up the remarkable body of a motion-picture. film.

On the length of time it was taking to make *The Treasure of the Sierra Madre:*

If that son of a bitch doesn't find water soon, I'll go broke.

Writers?

Voltaire, Voltaire, all these writers want to be Voltaire.

The boss:

Does anyone mind if I say a few words? Who's going to fire me if I do?

Someday somebody's going to have to figure out a way to give a farewell dinner to a conglomerate.

On typecasting:

No, no! Jimmy Stewart for Governor—Reagan for his best friend!

It was Jack's brother Harry Warner who made two classic statements.
On the introduction of sound:

Who the hell wants to hear actors talk?

On a bothersome producer, said to be Adolph Zukor:

Never let that bastard back in here—unless we need him!

DARRYL F. ZANUCK

Darryl F. Zanuck, born in 1902, can boast a long, controversial career in the film business. In 1933, he formed Twentieth Century, which later amalgamated with the Fox corporation, where he oversaw the production of the Shirley Temple movies and such quality features as *The Grapes of Wrath* (1940) and *All About Eve* (1950). As an independent, he took pride in his blockbuster, *The Longest Day* (1962). He then returned to Twentieth Century-Fox. When he was ousted in 1969, the company was renamed Twenty-First Century-Fox.

I'm the only studio president who's been a producer, a director, a writer, and an editor. Who knows the goddamn business better?

A motion picture lives three months at most. There is no use pretending we are making pictures for the ages.

There's nothing wrong with this business that good pictures won't cure.

The successful picture, big or small, has to make you do one of three things. Sit on the edge of your seat, laugh a lot or reach for your handkerchief. I used to have a gag man who claimed there were only two kinds of films. Slouch and sit up.

An executive cannot expect love—ever.

Goddamn it to hell. Don't threaten me! People don't threaten me. I threaten them!

It turned out to be one of my worst successes!

Writers are idiots with Underwoods.

And then I decided to become a genius.

Depth, we don't need depth! What we need is just one thing, a screen as big as the TV screen is small.

When a whore plays a whore in front of the man she loves—that is not tragic. When a decent girl plays a whore, then it is tragic.

Any of my indiscretions were with people, not actresses.

For God's sake, don't say yes until I've finished talking.

CLOSE-UPS

Darryl, if it were mine, I'd cut it up and sell it for mandolin picks. — Arthur Caesar

When I die, I want to be cremated and have my ashes sprinkled on Mr. Zanuck's driveway—so his car won't skid. — George Oppenheimer

Well, goodbye, Mr. Zanuck. And let me tell you, it certainly has been a pleasure working at Sixteenth Century-Fox. — Jean Renoir

One time I saw Darryl Zanuck in Pamplona watching a bullfight. It started to rain. Everyone left the arena except Zanuck. He sat there, and his cigar did not go out. God does not rain on Darryl Zanuck. — Kenneth Tynan

A ROSTER OF PRODUCERS

BUDDY ADLER:
We're dealing in illusion, and when the Elizabeth Taylors and Marilyn Monroes start to think and want to live normal lives like everyone else, soon we won't have any illusions left to sell.

DORE ASHTON:
Lana Turner had mixed feelings about it—she hated it and she detested it.

STEVE BROIDY:
The only positive thing in the motion picture business is the negative.

ART COHN:
When truth and friendship were at odds, I chose truth in the name of friendship.

DINO DI LAURENTIS:

The story for me is the star.

I've made lots of money in the business of making the audience my only boss.

Good God, Mayer! You know that my name was to be as large or larger than that of anyone else in connection with this picture, certainly larger than Tolstoy's.

No one cry when Jaws die. But when the monkey die, people gonna cry. Intellectuals gonna love Kong; even film buffs who love the first Kong gonna love ours.

I'm predicting that my electronic gorilla will win an Academy Award for the best acting performance of the year.

ROBERT EVANS:

The making of a blockbuster is the newest art form of the Twentieth Century.

Success is my companion.

WILLIAM FOX:

I don't think that there will ever be the much-dreamed-of talking pictures on a large scale. To have conversation would strain the eyesight and the sense of hearing at once, taking away the restfulness one gets from viewing pictures.

WILLIAM GOETZ:

If everyone who owns a Van Gogh goes to see the picture, it should be very successful.

SIR LEW GRADE:

The trouble with this business is that the stars keep ninety per cent of the money I earn.

HOWARD HUGHES:

We're not getting enough production out of Jane's breasts.

Eight million dollars? Do you realize that's a small fortune?

A close friend of Hughes', Yvonne De Carlo, explained how he introduced beautiful actresses to his great passion, flying:

Howard Hughes taught me to land a plane and how to take off. But he never taught me anything about the flying in between. He thought that I had learned the difficult parts, and that was enough.

ROSS HUNTER:

I don't want to hold a mirror up to life as it is. I just want to show the part that is attractive—not freckled faces and broken teeth but smooth faces and pearly white teeth.

121

What I offer people is escape. I have never in my life made a picture to please me. Can you imagine I'd make a film like Tammy for me?

JOHNNY HYDE:

When you're a failure in Hollywood—that's like starving to death outside a banquet hall with the smells of filet mignon driving you crazy.

HERBERT JAFFE:

We laughingly call ourselves an art-form, but our problems are the problems of any manufacturer.

LEO JAFFE:

From our standpoint, the prime objective is to make the customer feel that motion pictures are still one of the least expensive forms of entertainment.

JOSEPH P. KENNEDY:

Look at that bunch of pants-pressers in Hollywood making themselves millions.

EDWIN H. KNOPF:

The son-in-law also rises.

[A pun on the title of Hemingway's novel and the rise of David O. Selznick at MGM, operated by Selznick's father-in-law, Louis B. Mayer.]

SIR ALEXANDER KORDA:

It is not enough to be Hungarian—you have to have talent too.

CARL LAEMMLE:

All right! You can have a quartet—but don't get too many!

We kow-tow to Public Opinion—the one infallible censor.

JESSIE LASKY:

The producer must be a prophet and a general, a diplomat and a peacemaker, a miser and a spendthrift. He must have vision tempered by hindsight, daring governed by caution, the patience of a saint and the iron of a Cromwell.

JOSEPH E. LEVINE:

The film business is composed of an indescribable collection of dreamers and schemers, geniuses and phonies, sharpshooters and lunatics. It's action, on the screen and off.

I made it into a cocktail picture. You know what a cocktail picture is? That's a picture people talk about at cocktail parties. Nobody understood it. They just talked about it.

EDWARD J. MANNIX:

You know, I went around the world last year. And you want to know something? It hates each other!

DAVID MERRICK:

They call me the Mickey Spillane of Shubert Alley.

JOE PASTERNAK:

The big problem in Hollywood today is replacement. All the big stars are on crutches. You get a young girl falling in love with Cary Grant. In real life, she sleeps with him once or twice to see what it's like, then she leaves him. In Hollywood, they live happily ever after.

J. ARTHUR RANK:

I believe the best way we can spread the Gospel of Christ is through films.

HARRY RAPF:

Take out the essentials, and what have you got?

This is the best apple pie I ever had in my whole mouth.

DORE SCHARY:

America is a "happy-ending" nation.

JOSEPH M. SCHENCK:

We are not stalling, just procrastinating.

My father once told me that if you are cold sober and haven't had a drink in weeks and five sane and intelligent people look at you and tell you you are dead drunk, the best thing to do is not to argue but lie down and take a nap for an hour.

Charles K. Feldman once said of Schenck:

Joseph Schenck was the best poker player in Hollywood. You could play Joe for pennies and lose ten million dollars.

Anita Loos added:

If Hollywood ever wants to film a supercolossal epic of its own, it couldn't do better than to settle for the private life of Joseph M. Schenck.

NICHOLAS M. SCHENCK:

How long is it good?

Never in my life have I seen so many unhappy men making a hundred thousand dollars a year.

SPYROS SKOURAS:

No mariner ever distinguished himself on a smooth sea.

I can't even sleep at night. I have to accomplish and achieve. I burn inside to do things, big things!

And Billy Wilder commented:

The only Greek tragedy I know is Spyros Skouras.

SAM SPIEGEL:
Fifty thousand dollars for your thoughts!

You make a star, you make a monster.

HUNT STROMBERG:
Boy's, I've got an idea. Let's fill the screen with tits.

Tits and sand sell pictures.

MIKE TODD:
Everybody's got two businesses, his own and show biz.

I've never been poor, only broke. Being poor is a frame of mind. Being broke is only a temporary situation.

Money is only important if you haven't got it.

I spend money as though I had it.

If you want to be a millionaire, live like one.

Life is a toy balloon among children armed with pins.

JACK VALENTI:
A tyrant first appears in the guise of a protector.

JERRY WALD:
People thought I was Sammy. Let me tell you something: Sammy Glick was a boy scout leader compared to Harry Cohn.

We must explore more of the closed rooms of human experience and personality: the half-light of evil, guilt, conscience.

Budd Schulberg, author of *What Makes Sammy Run*, cautioned:

It was not entirely fair of many Hollywood people to identify Sammy Glick with Jerry Wald to the exclusion of at least half a dozen other possibilities.

HAL B. WALLIS:
It is the producer's business to gauge his public; it is the star's business to trust the producer's judgment.

I wonder if this business will ever turn honest.

I am always aware, as the blank screen is filled in, of the medium's power to move and affect and shape and change.

WALTER WANGER, on Hollywood parties:

If you didn't take the young lady on your right upstairs between the soup and the entrée, you were considered a homosexual.

ANDY WARHOL:

The lighting is bad, the camera work's bad, the projection is bad, but the people are beautiful.

All current cinema is romantic, literary, historical, expressionistic, etc. Let us forget all this and consider, if you please: a pipe—a chair—a hand—an eye—a typewriter—a hat—a foot, etc., etc.

WILLIAM A. WELLMAN:

My contention has always been, get a director and a writer together, and let them alone. That's how the best pictures get made.

Epitaph for the directors who fell at the crossroads of the world; date, long ago: LEAVING IT TO POSTERITY TO KNOW THE TRUTH.

FRANK YABLANS:

Movies have become events. It's not unusual for a movie to capture the imagination of the whole country.

I don't like any confusion about who is running Paramount. The name is Yablans.

CESARE ZAVATTINI:

We must identify ourselves with what we are. The world is full of people thinking of myths.

ADOLPH ZUKOR:

The public is never wrong.

Look ahead a little and gamble a lot.

The best commercial word in our slogan is the word "clean."

The film industry is still in swaddling clothes. The great days lie in the future.

To historian Terry Ramsaye go the closing words:

This empire of the screen has many subjects, slaves, magicians, sheiks, dancing girls, princesses, grand viziers and emirs. Chief of them all is a certain philosophic little man from Hungary, silent and meek among his millions. His name is Zukor, first and last in the alphabet of screen fame.

The Directors

"If the cinema is an art," asks the writer John Russell Taylor, "who is the artist?" It may be argued that film-making, being a group effort, does not require the services of a single artist, but the myriad talents of scores of able performers and craftsmen. There is truth in this, but it might also be argued that, just as a strong army is weak without a strong general, a film, to be great or even good, requires the stamp or style of a single personality, the director's.

The *auteur* theory goes even further. As set forth by François Truffaut in France and popularized in the United States by Andrew Sarris, the "author theory" maintains that the individual director may be the author of the film, being the one person able to give a "meaningful coherence" to that work, in line with his previous work. Thus, the work of a director may be studied from film to film, as one appreciates the evolving style and concerns of a poet or novelist. To answer Taylor's question, the director is the artist of the cinema. It is possible the eleven directors singled out for treatment here would not agree with the "author theory," yet their work—their films—may be seen as contributions to screen entertainment, to genre film-making, or to the growing body of their own work. There are eleven here—all artists in any sense of the word.

MICHELANGELO ANTONIONI

Anxiety and alienation in modern urban life are the subjects of Michelangelo Antonioni's films. Born in Italy in 1912, he directed *L'Avventura* (1960) in Italy, *Blow-Up* (1966) in England, and *Zabriskie Point* (1969) in the United States.

> *Everything hurts.*
>
> *Anything can be easy, and anything can be hard.*
>
> *It can happen that films acquire meanings: that is to say, that the meanings appear afterwards.*
>
> *One could perhaps understand the moon, the universe, even the horizons of life—but man himself remains mysterious. Life is difficult. My films are true.*
>
> *The only thing that matters is experience.*

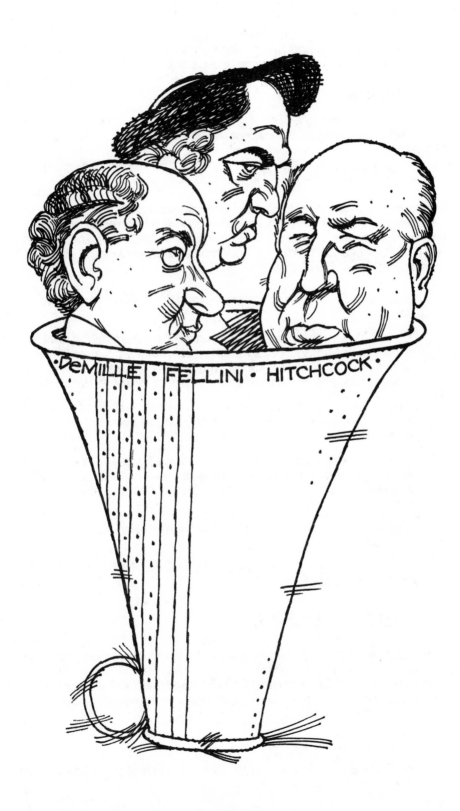

I feel that I am a person who has things that he wants to show, rather than things he wants to say. There are times when the two concepts coincide, and, then, we arrive at a work of art.

CLOSE-UP

Your pictures are like my paintings—about nothing, with precision.— Abstract expressionist painter, Mark Rothko

INGMAR BERGMAN

A stage director as well as a film director, Bergman was born in Sweden in 1918. The characters in his films are creatures stricken with guilt, remorse, and doubt. Among his many features are: *Smiles of a Summer Night* (1955), *The Seventh Seal* (1956), *Wild Strawberries* (1957), *Through a Glass Darkly* (1962), and *Cries and Whispers* (1972).

Stage work is very un-neurotic; film work is, shall we say, a little bit stressy.

I think it's terribly important that art exposes humiliation, that art shows how human beings humiliate each other, because humiliation is one of the most dreadful companions of humanity, and our whole social system is based to an enormous extent on humiliation.

We walk in circles, so limited by our own anxieties that we can no longer distinguish between true and false, between the gangster's whim and the purest ideal.

People ask what are my intentions with my films—my aims. It is a difficult and dangerous question, and I usually give an evasive answer: I try to tell the truth about the human condition, the truth as I see it.

Whenever I am in doubt, I take refuge in the vision of a simple and pure love.

A film is a tapeworm, a tapeworm 2,500 metres long that sucks the life and spirit out of me.

CECIL B. DeMILLE

Cecil B. DeMille (1881-1959) was the independent producer *par excellence.* He produced some seventy features from *The Squaw Man* (1913) to *The Ten Commandments* (1956) and claimed the Holy Land and the Roman Empire as part of his territory. He made a cameo appearance as the archetypal director in *Sunset Boulevard* (1950).

The public is always right.

I will trade you forty gorgeously beautiful Hawaiian sunsets for one good sock in the jaw.

The way to make a film is to begin with an earthquake and work up to a climax.

Cue the Red Sea!

The Bible has been a bestseller for centuries. Why should I let two thousand years of publicity go to waste?

I do not abide by the belief, popular in certain quarters, that motion-picture stories should be told to fit an audience level of ten or twelve years. This is a most erroneous concept.

Maybe the average Hollywood glamor-girl should be numbered instead of named.

I've taught you all I know...go and be a star.

Put that light back where it belongs.

I've owned this yacht since 1922, and there hasn't been an orgy on it yet!

It's harder to play a director than to be one.

Why shouldn't the bathroom express as much beauty as the drawing room?

The bath became a mystic shrine dedicated to Venus or, sometimes, to Apollo, and the art of bathing was shown as a lovely ceremony rather than a merely sanitary duty.

I believe that my pictures have had an obvious effect upon American life. I have brought a certain sense of beauty and luxury into everyday existence, all jokes about ornate bathrooms and deluxe boudoirs aside. I have done my bit toward lifting the level of daily life.

When the banks came into the picture, troubles came in with them. When we operated on our own money, there was joy in the industry. When we operated on Wall Street money, there was grief in the industry.

My next activity is in the hands of the Lord—and of Paramount.

My future plans? Another picture, I imagine. Or, perhaps, another world.

This is Cecil B. DeMille saying goodnight to you from Hollywood.

CLOSE-UPS

Cecil B. DeMille is indeed "Mr. Motion Picture." His films have brought something new to theaters. They call them customers. — Bob Hope

Cecil B. DeMille
Much against his will
Was persuaded to leave Moses
Out of the War of the Roses. — Caroline Lejeune

FEDERICO FELLINI

Frederico Fellini was born in Italy in 1920. There is a baroque quality about his films which has led one critic to call them "sentimental spectacles" and another to describe them as "grotesque tableaux." Three important Fellini films are: *La Strada* (1954), *La Dolce Vita* (1959), and *Fellini Satyricon* (1969).

Each of my stories is truly a season of my life.

I seem to be an image-producing machine.

One must invent everything.

All methods are legal.

The myths that must be destroyed are ideals in general. I think that the idealized life, idealized concepts, can be extremely dangerous for our mental health, and it is what I try to express in my films.

A good picture has to have defects. It has to have mistakes in it, like life, like people.

The artist is simply the medium between his fantasies and the rest of the world.

There is no end. There is no beginning. There is only the infinite passion of life.

My pictures never end.

CLOSE-UP

La Dolce Vita can play havoc with one's cavities.— Raoul Levy

JOHN FORD

A great feeling for the land and plenty of outdoor action are two characteristics of the films of John Ford (1895-1973), the most American of directors. Among his notable films are *The Informer* (1935), *Stagecoach* (1939), *The Grapes of Wrath* (1941), *How Green Was My Valley* (1941), and *The Last Hurrah* (1958).

I'm not an artist. I make movies.

Don't ever forget what I'm going to tell you. Actors are crap.

It's just a job of work, that's all. . .you do the best you can. . .like the man digging the ditch who says, "I hope the ground is soft so that my pick digs deeper."

CLOSE-UPS

A megaphone has been to John Ford what the chisel was to Michelangelo: his life, his passion, his cross.— Frank Capra

There's one general premise: almost anything that any of us has done you can find in a John Ford film. — Sidney Lumet

D.W. GRIFFITH

Once called "a frontier scout" of the American cinema, David Wark Griffith (1875-1948) was active in the film business from 1908 to 1940. He worked on a grand scale and dominated the early silent period. He introduced to the screen Mary Pickford and Lillian Gish, among others. Among his many features are the two silent-film blockbusters, *Birth of a Nation* (1915) and *Intolerance* (1916).

I loved the whole world onto a twenty-foot screen. I was a greater discoverer than Columbus.

Suppose I had patented the fade-out. I would be drawing at least a million a year in royalties.

My task? Joseph Conrad said, "It is, before all, to make you see."

Move these ten thousand horses a trifle to the right. . .and that mob out there three feet forward.

Taken as drama, war is, in some ways, unsatisfactory.

People don't go to the movies to read.

Movies are written in sand. Applauded today, forgotten tomorrow. Last week the names on the signs were different. Next week they will be changed again.

We can't deal with opinions. All we can do is weave a little romance as pleasantly as we know how.

The Academy of Motion Picture Arts and Sciences? What art? What science?

The most important thing is humanity.

What you get is a living. What you give is life.

When motion pictures have created something to compare with the plays of Euripides, or the work of Homer or Shakespeare or Ibsen, or the music of Handel or Bach, then let us call motion-picture entertainment an art—but not before then.

CLOSE-UPS

No one matches Griffith. He was, indeed, the poor man's Shakespeare. — Frank Capra

The naiveté of Griffith is just as great as the decadence of Bergman or Fellini. — Anita Loos

David Wark Griffith. Conjure with that name. Enshrine it. For no other has surpassed it since he shot Birth of a Nation. *Even though he worked with inferior tools, as did Michelangelo.*

—Adele Rogers St. Johns

D.W. Griffith? He was my day school, my adult-education program, my university.—Mack Sennett

ALFRED HITCHCOCK

Born in England in 1899, Alfred Hitchcock has worked in films since 1922, and in Hollywood itself since 1940. Among his taut, well-made thrillers are such favorites as *The Thirty-Nine Steps* (1935), *Rebecca* (1940), *North by Northwest* (1959), and *Psycho* (1960). It's fashionable to read into his films many philosophical messages.

Some films are slices of life. Mine are slices of cake.

If I make a film of Cinderella, people will immediately start looking for the corpse.

The only thing wrong with the silent film was the fact that people opened their mouths and no sound came out.

A good film is when the price of the dinner, the theater admission, and the babysitter were worth it.

In feature films the director is God; in documentary films God is the director.

I have a little phrase of my own. I always say logic is dull.

What is horror? It is a matter of taste—and I don't mean the blood.

The chase seems to me the final expression of the motion-picture medium.

Television has brought murder back into the home—where it belongs.

I always say that the most difficult things to photograph are dogs, babies, motorboats, Charles Laughton (God rest his soul), and method actors.

Actors? Cattle.

I deny I ever said that actors are cattle. What I said was, "Actors should be treated like cattle."

The best screen actor is the man who can do nothing extremely well.

What is drama but life with the dull bits cut out?

When we make films for the United States, we are automatically making them for all the world—because America is full of foreigners.

Hitchcock uses a lot of skill over a lot of nothing.— James Agee

JOHN HUSTON

King Rebel is the title of a biography of John Huston. Most would agree that the title is apt and would be tempted to add the word "maverick." Born in 1906, Huston made his directorial debut with *The Maltese Falcon* (1941) and went on to direct *The Treasure of the Sierra Madre* (1947) and *The African Queen* (1952). He narrated *Freud: The Secret Passion* (1962) and appeared as an actor in *Chinatown* (1974).

The cinema sees deep.

What you try to become is a bringer of magic. For magic and truth are closely allied, and movies are sheer magic.

What you see on the screen aren't people. They're shadows, gods and goddesses who don't have a third side, a human dimension. The screen is a myth and should be made of heroes and heroines.

The director is the actor's sole audience.

Fear makes you run one way—courage makes you run the other.

Fine. I've always known that girls have breasts.

The Maltese Falcon was produced three times before I did it, but never with very much success, so I decided on a radical procedure: to follow the book rather than depart from it. This was practically an unheard of thing to do with any picture taken from a novel, and marks the beginning of a great epoch in picture making.

You need about twenty million dollars to live properly. My life span would probably be lengthened if I had that much. It's only trying to make twenty million dollars that cuts short a man's years. Spending it would be healthy.

Hollywood has always been a cage, a cage to catch our dreams.

Each film is a little lifetime.

JEAN RENOIR

The great French director Jean Renoir (1894-1979) knew how to mingle—in a magisterial way—Pathos and Chaos. Among his feature films are: *La Grande Illusion* (1937), *La Règle du Jeu* (1939), and *The River* (1951).

Masterpieces are made by artisans, not artists.

My secret is not to consider myself as a director but as a midwife.

The calling I seek to practise has nothing to do with the film industry.

To the question: "Is the cinema an art?" my answer is: "What does it matter?" You can make films or you can cultivate a garden.

Everything that moves on the screen is cinema.

We must never forget the bistro in Magagnosc.

The advantage of being eighty years old is that one has had many people to love.

Today, the new being that I am realizes that it is no longer time for sarcasm and that the only thing I can bring to this illogical, irresponsible and cruel universe is my love.

I hate brains. I like the senses.

Life itself is an infinitely more rewarding spectacle than all the inventions of the mind.

A little mystery in the cinema, or in life for that matter, does no harm.

Imagination is the thing to be afraid of.

CLOSE-UP

Renoir has a lot of talent, but he's not one of us. — Darryl F. Zanuck

ORSON WELLES

Orson Welles, born in 1915, has created many cinematic moments of great originality. His first two features, *Citizen Kane* (1941) and *The Magnificent Ambersons* (1942), are among the screen's masterworks. His presence as an actor is overpowering—witness his role as Harry Lime in *The Third Man* (1949).

I am not free, my necessities are just different from yours.

A film is never really good unless the camera is an eye in the head of a poet.

A movie studio is the best toy a boy ever had.

The cinema has no boundary; it is a ribbon of dreams.

The camera is much more than a recording apparatus. It is a medium via which messages reach us from another world.

Every actor in his heart believes everything bad that's printed about him.

I began at the top and I've been working my way down ever since.

I've been given the use of my tools exactly eight times in twenty years.

We should have the courage of our platitudes.

I drag my myth around with me.

There is in Orson Welles a curious mixture of barbarism, cunning, childishness, and poetic genius.— André Bazin

Orson Welles is a kind of giant with a child-like face, a tree filled with birds and shadows, a dog who has snapped his chain and lies in the flowerbeds, an active idler, a wise fool, isolation surrounded by humanity, a student who dozes in class, a strategist who pretends to be drunk when he wants to be left in peace.— Jean Cocteau

BILLY WILDER

Born in Vienna in 1906, Billy Wilder was a writer before he was a director; consequently, his films are marked by a highly literate stamp. He co-wrote *Ninotchka* (1939) and directed a host of features, including *Double Indemnity* (1944), *Sunset Boulevard* (1950), *Some Like It Hot* (1959), and *Fedora* (1979).

I have a vast and terrible desire never to bore.

All I try to do is to get myself a story, splash it on the screen, and get it over with.

I have a healthy aunt in Vienna who would come on set on time, know her lines, and always be ready. But no one would pay to see her at the box office.

I do not believe in wasting money. On the other hand, nobody is going to go and see a picture simply because it came in under budget.

Make the subtleties obvious.

Hindsight is always twenty-twenty.

My pictures are not intended to reform people. Hopefully, they are stories sufficiently intriguing to make them forget the popcorn.

I'd worship the ground you walked on if only you lived in a better neighborhood.

Keep it out of focus. I want to win the foreign-picture award.

CLOSE-UP

Beneath Billy Wilder's aggressive gruff exterior is pure Brillo.
— Harry Kurnitz

A CAST OF DIRECTORS

ROBERT ALDRICH:
A director is a ringmaster, a psychiatrist, and a referee.

ROBERT ALTMAN:

Nobody has ever made a good movie. Someday, someone will make half a good one.

LINDSAY ANDERSON:

We're all overpaid. There are people digging coal who should be making more money than Elizabeth Taylor, but nothing's fair anymore.

KENNETH ANGER:

My films cause things to happen. They're not mere cinematic decoration.

Overnight the obscure and somewhat disreputable movie performers found themselves propelled to adulation, fame and fortune. They were the new royalty, the Golden People.

ALEXANDRE ASTRUC:

For me subjects are no more than pretexts. I can project into almost any story those things which are dear to my heart.

The fundamental problem of the cinema is how to express thought.

BERNARDO BERTOLUCCI:

It would be proper to put the name of my analyst in the credits of my films.

Pornography is not in the hands of the child who discovers his sexuality by masturbating, but in the hands of the adult who slaps him.

PETER BOGDANOVICH:

Don't you think the criterion for judging whether or not a picture is artistically sucessful is time?

STAN BRAKHAGE:

I see the intellect as always in charge of and charged by feeling.

ROBERT BRESSON:

A film is not a spectacle, it is pre-eminently a style.

I believe it is good to create obstacles.

There must, at a certain moment, be a transformation; if not, there is no art.

MEL BROOKS:

I stare at life through fields of mayonnaise.

Suppose I became the Jean Renoir of America. What the hell would be left for the other guys to do?

Bad taste is simply saying the truth before it should be said.

CLARENCE BROWN:

We were all right in the old days before the relatives got in as producers.

LUIS BUÑUEL:

Mystery is the essential element in every work of art. I shall never tire of repeating this.

I make movies to show that this is not the best of all possible worlds.

Bourgeois morality is for me immoral, and to be fought.

Nothing, *in this film,* symbolizes anything. *I ask that a film* discover *something for me.*

Thank God I am still an atheist.

FRANK CAPRA:

Directors have the power to speak to hundreds of millions for two hours—and in the dark.

Movies made here have Americanized the world.

My measure for all things was simple: Was it good for Frank Capra?

In short: "The audience is always right" is a safe bet.

There are no rules in film-making, only sins. And the cardinal sin is Dullness.

Garson Kanin, the film writer, once said:

I'd rather be Capra than God. If there is a Capra.

JOHN CASSAVETES:

I never know what my movies are about until I finish them.

ALBERTO CAVALCANTI:

The camera is so literal-minded that if you show it actors dressed up, it sees actors dressed up, not characters.

CLAUDE CHABROL:

There is no New Wave; there is only the sea.

Foolishness is infinitely more fascinating than intelligence, infinitely more profound. Intelligence has limits while foolishness has none.

RENÉ CLAIR:

If there is an aesthetics of the cinema. . . it can be summarized in one word: "Movement."

I never should have given up opium.

HENRI-GEORGES CLOUZOT:

I want to delight the little child who sleeps in our hearts—the child who hides her head under the bed covers and begs, "Daddy, Daddy frighten me!"

JEAN COCTEAU:

It is not up to us to obey the public which does not know what it wants, but to compel the public to follow us. If it refuses, we must use tricks: images, stars, décors and other magic lanterns, suitable to intrigue children and make them swallow the spectacle.

Since these mysteries exceed my grasp, I shall pretend to have organized them.

After forty, we are responsible for our own faces.

Cinemascope? The next time I write a poem, I shall use a larger piece of paper.

MERIAN C. COOPER, co-producer of *King Kong*:

I told Fay Wray she would have as her leading man the tallest, darkest man in Hollywood.

FRANCIS FORD COPPOLA:

You don't make films on anything but money—and whatever talent you can bring to them.

But imagine! Going to a movie for three hours and having every part of you touched in some profound, overwhelming way.

COSTA-GAVRAS:

Editing is the most important point in a picture; it is the director, really writing the picture with his editing.

GEORGE CUKOR:

Personally, I adore clothes. I think they're one of the better inventions of mankind.

Real talent is a mystery, and people who've got it know it.

Give me a good script, and I'll be a hundred times better as a director.

I'm full of curiosity! And I have an almost mystical respect for other people's talent.

MICHAEL CURTIZ—like Sam Goldwyn, a touch of Mrs. Malaprop:

The next time I send a fool for something, I go myself.

When I see the pictures you play in that theater, it makes the hair stand on the edge of my seat.

You think I know fuck nothing. . . well, let me tell you—I know fuck all!

This scene will make your blood curl.

Please stand a little closer apart.

That artificial skating rink is the real thing.

I don't see black and white words in script when I read it. I see action!

Okay, bring on the empty horses.

VITTORIO DE SICA:
What does the method of working matter as long as the result obtained is both poetic and true.

There is always an excuse, even for the criminal. Humanity is a very deep mystery.

ALEXANDER DOVZHENKO:
God exists. But his name is chance.

CARL DREYER:
Nothing in the world can be compared to the human face. It is a land one can never tire of exploring.

Imagine that we are sitting in an ordinary room. Suddenly we are told that there is a corpse behind the door. In an instant the room we are sitting in is completely altered: everything in it has taken on another look; the light, the atmosphere have changed, though they are physically the same. This is because we have changed, and the objects are as we conceive them. That is the effect I want to get in my film.

The essential is sufficient.

ALLAN DWAN:
If you get your head above the mob, they try to knock it off. If you stay down, you last forever.

SERGEI EISENSTEIN:
A collar button under a lens and thrown on a screen may become a radiant planet.

JEAN EPSTEIN:
There are no stories. There have never been stories. There are only situations without tail or head; without beginning, center, and end.

RAINER WERNER FASSBINDER:
Christianity is a wonderful thing, but the churches should be blown up.

ROBERT FLAHERTY:
First I am an explorer, and only then am I an artist.

VICTOR FLEMING:

I don't want to move in, goddamn it! I don't want to move the camera. Let the people do it, not the camera.

GEORGES FRANJU:

One can be ambiguous in one's sentiments, but not in the expression one gives them. In the depiction of one's sentiments, one must be clear, direct.

The Nouvelle Vague? There's a film to make about that. I've already got the title: Low Tide.

JOHN FRANKENHEIMER:

There doesn't seem to be room for the qualified success.

There seems to be a mysterious underground that lets people know in advance if a picture will be a hit. Thereafter, the successful movie seems to take on a life of its own.

ABEL GANCE:

My greatest mistake was ever to have compromised. My greatest achievement has been to survive.

JEAN-LUC GODARD:

Film is truth twenty-four times a second.

Truth is in all things, even, partly, in error.

On our modest scale we, too, must create two or three Vietnams in the heart of the immense Hollywood-Cinecitta-Mosfilms-Pinewood, etc., empire.

What I want above all is to destroy the idea of culture.

Instead of writing criticism, I now film it.

A film is the world in an hour and a half.

JOSH GREENFELD:

Directors are people too short to be actors.

JOHN GRIERSON:

In documentary, you do not shoot with your head only, but also with your stomach muscles.

When a director dies—he becomes a cameraman.

CURTIS HARRINGTON:

There are no primitives behind a camera lens.

HOWARD HAWKS:

I love to copy... myself.

WERNER HERZOG:
Film is not the art of scholars but of illiterates.

NORMAN JEWISON:
Films can have a tremendous impact upon us because they show us how life can be if we're not careful.

ALEXANDRO JODOROWSKY:
I demand of a film what many North Americans demand of drugs.

NUNNALLY JOHNSON:
Let's show the movies in the street—and drive the people back into the theaters.

ELIA KAZAN:
My real problem has not been with stupid producers or with the "front office." It has been with myself.

HENRY KING:
I try to tell a story in action rather than words, to eliminate everything in the script that can be told without words.

TED KOTCHEFF:
In the future I think they're going to give you an Oscar just for finishing a film.

STANLEY KRAMER:
In the American film, the economics are so strange that from the moment you pick up a piece of material you write down $1,000,000 in the left-hand column. Which is never seen on the screen.

STANLEY KUBRICK:
If you can talk brilliantly about a problem, it can create the consoling illusion that it has been mastered.

The great nations have always acted like gangsters, and the small nations like prostitutes.

AKIRA KUROSAWA:
I keep saying the same thing in different ways: If I look at the pictures I've made, I think they say, "Why is it that human beings aren't happy?"

I wanted to make a film which would be entertaining enough to eat.

FRITZ LANG:
It has become much more important to make money with pictures than to make pictures that make money. Every good picture will make money, but since the business interests took over, the business went down hill.

When I shot the take-off, I said, "If I count one, two, three, four, ten, fifty, hundred—an audience doesn't know when it will go off. But if I count down—ten, nine, eight, seven, six, five, four, three, two, one, ZERO!—Then they will know." Thus the countdown.

Love has become a four-letter word.

Directors are often blamed: "Why did you do this? And why did you do that?" But nobody ever says: "Even a director has to eat."

CLAUDE LELOUCH:

My films are for a world in which the concept of "alienation" has all but replaced that of "love." If the audience can experience joy—though vicarious—in response to them, then I will feel that I have been a success.

I make films the way I make love. I think it is a mistake for a director to trust someone else with the camera work. It's as though Van Gogh might have given his brush to someone else.

DAVID LEAN:

There's a tendency to think that if a film is expensive, it's going to be an artistic failure.

MERVYN LE ROY:

Second chances are as rare in Hollywood as ski tows.

If Shakespeare were writing **Hamlet** for me, I'd make him cut a lot of those speeches—too long.

In Hollywood, there are ways to manufacture beauty; you can't manufacture talent.

You don't photograph the money, you photograph the story.

Let's not improve this into a flop.

Mister Bastard, if you please!

Today's films are made too fast and too dirty and cost either too much or too little.

I consider myself a typical member of the audience.

I can honestly say that I never made a picture I didn't like.

ALBERT LEWIN:

In England, you could have all the cleavage you wanted but no violence. Over here, you couldn't have any cleavage, but you could have violence.

I always tried to make pictures that would please me and some of my intelligent friends and still please the general public enough to pay off and make some money. On the whole, I got away with it.

JOSEPH LOSEY:

Films have become a matter of mergers and real estate.

I feel very strongly that no film is worth much attention unless it has what I call a signature.

Film is a dog: The head is commerce; the tail is art. And only rarely does the tail wag the dog.

ERNST LUBITSCH:

There are a thousand ways to point a camera, but really only one.

The American public—with the mind of a twelve-year-old child, you know—it must have life as it ain't.

All women are sirens at heart.

SIDNEY LUMET:

If you care about your work, every frame matters.

Directors are no different than anybody else; their capacity for self-deception is enormous.

LOUIS MALLE:

For me, film is a fantastic means of investigation. You see the world much better through a camera.

JOSEPH L. MANKIEWICZ:

If the court please, the box office isn't an opinion, it's a fact.

LOTHAR MENDES:

When they yell "Camera!" it means relax.

RUSS MEYER:

I deal in big bosoms and square jaws.

LEWIS MILESTONE:

I've got your happy ending. We'll let the Germans win the war.

KENJI MIZOGUCHI:

I think the true work of an artist can only be accomplished after he is fifty, when he has enriched his life with accumulated experiences.

PAUL MORRISSEY:

When Andy Warhol started making movies, he went all the way back to Edison. The only thing he could do was move forward.

F.W. MURNAU:

The camera is the director's sketching pencil. It should be as mobile as possible to catch every passing mood, and it is important that the camera should not be interposed between the spectator and the picture.

JEAN NEGULESCO:

You move when things get static; that's the secret of picture-making.

MIKE NICHOLS:

Nothing trains you for life.

You have to go on as yourself.

MAX OPHULS:

The early film makers were the first adventurers of the imagination. What they photographed were the first dreams, the first kisses, the first fires and the first waters, the first war and the first peace, the first birth and the first death. What they shot was the first shooting.

MARCEL PAGNOL:

Any man who has served in the Turkish Navy can't help knowing about films.

GABRIEL PASCAL:

Vestal virgins half-nude in a steambath. That is Hollywood's idea of sex. They must think the American male is so tired and impotent that he has to have a vast exposure of female flesh to excite him.

JOE PASTERNAK:

You call this a script? Give me a couple of $5,000-a-week writers and I'll write it myself!

ROMAN POLANSKI:

Sometimes I'm charmed by the fact that there are women with whom you can discuss the molecular theory of light all evening, and at the end they will ask you what is your birth sign.

We are born; it means nothing; we die.

OTTO PREMINGER:

My reputation for firing people is all the product of publicity. I am a sweet, lovable, gentle man.

I see it as "Otto Preminger's Exodus."

Fellow director Billy Wilder quipped:

I'm sorry, but I wouldn't dare disagree with Otto Preminger. I still have relatives in Germany.

V.I. PUDOVKIN:

The film is the greatest teacher because it teaches not only through the brain but through the whole body.

The film is not shot, but built, built up from the separate strips of celluloid that are its raw material.

Theorist Aram Avakian added:

> When you're editing, nobody else knows what you're doing except Pudovkin's ghost.

GREGORY RATOFF—a malapropist of sorts:
> For your information, just answer me one question.

> You are a parasite for sore eyes.

> Vegetables are my meat.

> It's a great role, and you'll play it to the tilt.

> John Huston, if you weren't the son of my beloved friend Walter, and if you weren't a brilliant writer and a magnificent director, you'd be nothing but a common drunk.

Producer Darryl F. Zanuck threatened to add the following credit-line to one of his own movies:

> Based on a remark by Gregory Ratoff.

NICHOLAS RAY:
> There is no theater in America today, except in the courtrooms and the railroad stations.

> There is no formula for success. But there is a formula for failure and that is to try to please everybody.

SATYAJIT RAY:
> They usually show my films in Delhi at eight o'clock on Sunday morning.

CAROL REED:
> If the purpose is to make the audience laugh, cry, be excited or frightened, then the greatest quality a film can have is the sense of the precise rightness in the means used to that end.

ALAIN RESNAIS:
> I don't mold people's reactions; I create a hollow they can put their feelings into.

> I believe that an influence ceases when the person receiving it becomes aware of it.

LENI RIEFENSTAHL:
> I filmed the truth as it was then. Nothing more.

> I told Hitler I didn't know what is SS or what is SA.

ERIC ROHMER:
> All women are the same. It's the intellect that counts.

ROBERTO ROSSELLINI:

My primary aim is to recapture the tremendous innocence of the original glance, the very first image that apppeared to our eyes.

One makes films in order to become a better human being.

KEN RUSSELL:

What the public wants is sex and violence.

That's very unfortunate because if we take out all the pubic hair, there won't be much left to the movies, will there?

Film-making is an odyssey. You never know what is going to happen. You set out on a journey, meet all sorts of monsters on the way, and, in the end, you either win or get wounded.

DON SIEGEL:

If you start at the top and work your way down to the bottom, at least you've been at the top.

GEORGE STEVENS:

CinemaScope is fine if you want a system that shows a boa constrictor to better advantage than a man.

When the camera is whirring, you're mining your vein. When it isn't whirring—nothing.

JOHN STURGES:

You can't go around the theaters handing out cards saying, "It isn't my fault." You go on to the next one.

I was a director. Whether I was good or bad was beside the point.

FRANÇOIS TRUFFAUT:

The film of tomorrow seems to me even more personal than a novel, individual and autobiographical, like a confession or a private diary.

When I make a film, the world is divided into two parts—that which is good for the movie and that which is not.

ROGER VADIM:

The problem is to make the woman know that she wants you.

STAN VANDERBEEK:

Motion pictures…are simply the most complete form imaginable for an artist to work in.

AGNES VARDA:

In my films I always wanted to make people see deeply. I don't want to show things, but to give people the desire to see.

DZIGA VERTOV:

Down with the bourgeois tale scenario! Hurrah for life as it is!

KING VIDOR:

The picture was so bad they had to do retakes before they could put it on the shelf.

LUCHINO VISCONTI:

I could make a film in front of a blank wall if I were sure of finding the real human elements of the character placed in front of this bare décor.

JOSEF VON STERNBERG:

The illusion of reality is what I look for, not reality itself.

I am ice cold. You cannot direct unless you have contempt for your camera, contempt for your lights, contempt for your actors.

The very opposite of the scarecrow is the actor: his function is to attract—he frightens no one but himself.

A camera has been present at the birth of a child and at the death of a tsar. Directly or obliquely, everything on earth has been funnelled into celluloid, and somewhere, in back of the lens through which all this had to pass was a director.

You can seduce a man's wife here, attack his daughter, and wipe your hands on his canary bird; if you don't like his movie, you're dead.

Somewhere in my subconscious mind I have a sort of photographic place. I see everything in the form of a scene for a picture.

One hundred thousand dollars? Is that all? I think they are trying to humiliate me.

No, not ten years ahead. I was twenty years ahead of my time.

EDGAR G. ULMER:

I really am looking for absolution for all the things I had to do for money's sake.

RAOUL WALSH:

Actors and actresses used to come dressed up for interviews; now they show up in sweat shirts and jock-straps!

LINA WERTMULLER:

I am a terrified optimist.

MICHAEL WINNER:

If you want art, don't mess around with movies—buy a Picasso.

The Writers

No story ever written for the screen is as dramatic as the story of the screen—Will H. Hayes.

Writers came into their own when the motion pictures learned to talk. Suddenly, in the late Twenties, audiences were called upon to do more than stare at the screen and guess at the words the actors were mouthing. Now they were actually listening to the words as the actors were speaking them.

With the new words, came the writers able to string them out in photoplays, scenarios, screenplays, and scripts. Some of Hollywood's best lines come from the early Thirties, when the producers and directors and screen writers were exploring their new-found mode of expression: dialogue. This freedom brought to Hollywood some of the ablest of wordsmiths, who were often the most incisive wits of the period. They worked under "the moguls," who from the Thirties to the Fifties ruled the big studios, paid the bills, produced the features, and (with Harry Cohn and Louis B. Mayer, at least) had no time for honeyed words or delicate ironies.

Many of the important wordsmiths are quoted in this chapter. First come the "Screen Writers." Many of them are better-known for other accomplishments, but all of them have written, or adapted original screen plays or properties. Then come "Writers and Artists": novelists and poets and others who have something to add, usually in choice words and strong sentences. They are followed by the "Thinkers and Theorists" who addressed their experience and intelligence to some of the philosophical questions raised by the cinema. Finally, there appear the people who usually have the last word—the reviewers, critics, columnists, correspondents, and journalists who compose "Critics and Innocent Bystanders."

Very often, what stands out in this chapter is not so much the wordsmiths' words on art as it is their art with words, which, perhaps, is as it should be.

SCREEN WRITERS

RAY BRADBURY:
There is my script, my new and inevitable FINIS. Film it in your mind. Screen it on your eyelids tonight.

ROBERT BENCHLEY:
The biggest obstacle to professional writing is the necessity for changing a typewriter ribbon.

IRVING BRECHER, on wide screens:

Why not keep the theater screens the same size and simply reduce the size of the audience?

ARTHUR CAESAR, on being a yes man:

I don't want to be right: I just want to keep on working.

BORDEN CHASE, on the new morality:

Now a kid comes out of college and writes a screenplay, bless his heart. But I wonder what will happen when pornography goes out of style.

RAYMOND CHANDLER:

If my books had been any worse, I should not have been invited to Hollywood, and if they had been any better, I should not have come.

Why am I doing it?. . . partly because one gets tired of saying no, and some day I might want to say yes and not get asked.

LENORE COFFEE:

When a man of forty falls in love with a girl of twenty, it isn't her youth he is seeking but his own.

HOWARD DIETZ:

Being useful is a good way to make friends.

A list of those who visited my house at various times sounded like "Who's Who." The names were so heavy you couldn't fail to drop them.

I went to the Algonquin and watched the Round Table eat.

PHILIP DUNNE:

A screenwriter at best is a stylistic chameleon: he writes in the style of the original source—or should, if he's worth his salt.

WILLIAM FAULKNER:

I don't like scenario writing because I don't know enough about it.

She tried to sit in my lap while I was standing up.

Boy meets girl. . . boy gets girl. . . boy loses girl. . . boy sues girl. . . .

Can I work at home?

JULES FEIFFER:

Good swiping is an art in itself.

F. SCOTT FITZGERALD:

As long past as 1930, I had a hunch that the talkies would make even the best-selling novelist as archaic as silent pictures.

ELINOR GLYN, creator of "It":

To define a man: he must be a creature who makes me feel that I am a woman.

I had not been long in Hollywood before I discovered that what I had always suspected was true. American men, in those days, could not make love.

Oh, that is my word. It! Don't you see, that one syllable expresses everything—all the difference there is between people. You either have It or you haven't.

Whatever will bring in the most money will happen.

MOSS HART:

Star quality. It's that little something extra that Ellen Terry talked about.

BEN HECHT:

In Hollywood, a starlet is the name for any woman under thirty who is not actively employed in a brothel.

A movie is basically so trite and glib that the addition of a half-dozen miserable inanities does not cripple it.

CHRISTOPHER ISHERWOOD:

A screenwriter is a man who is being tortured to confess and has nothing to confess.

The film studio of today is really the palace of the sixteenth century. There one sees what Shakespeare saw: the absolute power of the tyrant, the courtiers, the flatterers, the jesters, the cunningly ambitious intriguers.

GARSON KANIN:

Every movie star is a leading character in a fairy tale.

A movie star is a creation that, like a painting or a statue or a symphony, does not age.

The past, recalled, is a flowing cornucopia of vision, sounds, aromas, emotions, gaieties, terrors, faces, and places.

ALEXANDER KING:

The films take our best ideas. We work like slaves, inventing, devising, changing, to please the morons who run this game. We spend endless hours in search of novel ideas, and, in the end, what do we get for it? A lousy fortune!

HOWARD W. KOCH:

Writing a screenplay in Hollywood, or anywhere else, is only part of a writer's function; struggling to preserve its values is the other part. If he cares enough, he'll do it.

HARRY KURNITZ:
> *In 1972 Stark Raving, the last screenwriter left in Hollywood, committed suicide by jumping into the dialog-mixer at Universal-International.*

> *The Hollywood version of the Twenty-third Psalm is "My pool runneth over."*

RING LARDNER:
> *If perchance the inevitable should come. . . .*

RING LARDNER, JR.:
> *I could answer your question, but I would hate myself in the morning.*

ARTHUR LAURENTS:
> *I wonder what would have happened to Romeo and Juliet if they had lived.*

> *The main character in any film is the camera—and that is created by the director.*

ISABEL LENNART:
> *I used to be prejudiced against directors, but now I'm bigoted against them.*

ANITA LOOS:
> *Gentlemen prefer blondes, but marry brunettes.*

> *Men no longer prefer blondes. Today gentlemen seem to prefer gentlemen.*

> *If we had to tell Hollywood goodbye, it may be with one of those tender, old-fashioned, seven-second kisses exchanged between two people of the opposite sex, with all their clothes on.*

> *I know many more men who are kept by women these days than I did women who were kept by men in the Twenties.*

> *Memory is more indelible than ink.*

> *A girl can't go on laughing all the time.*

> *Each one dances alone.*

PARRE LORENZ:
> *First, employ an honest and gifted writer—ONE—to write a shot. Do not change it. Employ a good director to make it. Give him enough money to employ expert craftsmen and talented actors. Selah! You have a good movie.*

WILLIAM LUDWIG, on the current state of Hollywood:
> *They should have kept the props and auctioned off the producers.*

CHARLES MacARTHUR:
> Complaints are only a sign you've been hurt. Keep the wounds out of sight.

HERMAN J. MANKIEWICZ:
> I know lots of $75-a-week writers, but they're all making $1,500 a week.

> It was very strange. All those empty sound stages, and the wind whistling down the studio street. I couldn't get rid of the feeling that, any minute, I'd look out and see tumbleweeds come rolling past.

JOSEPH L. MANKIEWICZ:
> Men react as they're taught to react, in what they've been taught is a "manly" way. Women are, by comparison, as if assembed by the wind.

> Antonioni—and Art? What epithets do we set aside for Aeschylus, Aristophanes, et al.?

> My films talk a lot—well, I talk a lot.

> A properly written screenplay has, in effect, already been directed.

WOLF MANKOWITZ:
> You can definitely say that my gall isn't divided into three parts.

FRANCES MARION, on deglamorization and the old Hollywood:
> The Sphinx loses its mystery in the noonday sun.

PAUL MAZURSKI:
> Richard Nixon is my President, Ronald Reagan is my Governor, George Murphy is my Senator, Sam Yorty is my Mayor, and the William Morris office is my agent—and you want to know why I'm depressed?

DUDLEY NICHOLS:
> A script is only a blueprint—the director is the one who makes the picture.

JAMES POE:
> The screenwriter is an architect, and the director is a contractor.

MORRIS RYSKIND:
> But then, stage, screen, or novel, no writer is completely sane.

BERNARD SLADE:
> A laugh is the reverse of a breakdown; it's a break up.

TERRY SOUTHERN:
> You've got to understand that it is not easy to make a bad movie—it requires a very special combination of talents and anti-talents.

DONALD OGDEN STEWART:

Try to find out who the star of your film will actually be. It's very disconcerting to have written something for Joan Crawford and find it's Lana Turner who'll be the actual star. Secondly, never tackle a screenplay at the beginning of its development. Let the producer and his other writers mess it up, and then, when they're faced with an actual shooting date, you do the final job. And, finally, you must learn not to let them break your heart.

DALTON TRUMBO:

The system under which writers work would sap the vitality of a Shakespeare. They are intelligent enough to know that they are writing trash but not intelligent enough to do anything about it.

CESAR ZAVATTINI:

I must tell reality as if it were a story; there must be no gap between life and what is on the screen.

The reality buried under the myths slowly reflowered. The cinema began its creation of the world. Here was a tree; here an old man; here a house; here a man eating, a man sleeping, a man crying. . . .

FERDINAND ZECCA:

I am rewriting Shakespeare. The wretched fellow has left out the most marvelous things.

AUTHORS AND ARTISTS

ELIZABETH BOWEN:

To get back to my star: I enjoy sitting opposite him or her, the delights of intimacy without the onus, high points of possession without strain.

TRUMAN CAPOTE:

I've known some actors who were intelligent, but the better the actor, the more stupid he is.

BLAISE CENDRARS:

The screen showed a crowd, and in this crowd there was a lad with his cap under his arm: suddenly this cap which was like all other caps began, without moving, to assume intense life; you felt it was all set to jump, like a leopard! Why, I don't know.

LEONARD COHEN:

I've always had a fantasy that some director will find me sitting in at a drug store counter, like Hedy Lamarr or whoever it was.

MALCOLM COWLEY:

After publishing an admired book, or two or three, the writer was offered a contract by a movie studio, then he bought a house with a 153 *swimming pool and vanished from print. If he reappeared years later, it was usually with a novel designed to have the deceptive appeal of an uplift brassiere.*

GRAHAM GREENE:

I wish there existed an organization with the means to anthologize the excellent sequences that can so often be found in the worst films and save them from oblivion.

For an actor, success is simply delayed failure.

JOHN CLELLON HOLMES:

One's boyhood experience of the Depression may center around a Hooverville or a house in the suburbs, but one's fantasies of those years are likely to inhabit that carefree world, as shiny and shallow as patent leather, where Fred Astaire and Ginger Rogers denied all shabbiness and anxiety for a few hypnotic hours.

ALDOUS HUXLEY:

What makes a star? It's the star's ability to hypnotize an entire mass audience, to reach out, to cast a spell.

X. J. KENNEDY:

The tragedy of King Kong, then, is to be the beast who, at the end of the fable, fails to turn into the handsome prince.

STEPHEN LEACOCK:

The muse Cinematographia is the sunken sister of the arts, beautiful but wicked. She will do anything for Money.

VACHEL LINDSAY:

I am the old poet who has a right to claim for . . . muses Blanche Sweet, Mary Pickford, and Mae Marsh.

NORMAN MAILER:

There is something sinister about film. Film is a phenomenon whose resemblance to death has been ignored for too long.

H.L. MENCKEN:

A movie actor's house is a series of movie sets, and he wears clothes that are hard to distinguish from his costumes.

And there will be movies made by artists, and for people who can read and write.

GEORGE JEAN NATHAN:

My interest in the cinema has lapsed since women began to talk.

ROBERT NATHAN:

I also learned, to my surprise, that a picture is not at all like a play; that, on the contrary, it is like a novel, but a novel to be seen, instead of told.

ALLARDYCE NICOLL:

If the theater stands thus for mankind, the cinema stands for the individual.

FRANK O'HARA:

The heavens operate on the star system. It is a divine precedent you perpetuate! Roll on, reels of celluloid, as the great earth rolls on!

And give credit where it's due. . . to you, glorious Silver Screen, tragic Technicolor, amorous CinemaScope, stretching Vistavision and startling Stereophonic Sound, with all your heavenly dimensions and reverberations and iconoclasms!

JOHN O'HARA:

Do yourself a favor. Go to your neighborhood exhibitor and ask him why he isn't showing Citizen Kane.

DOROTHY PARKER:

Hollywood money isn't money. It's congealed snow, melts in your hand, and there you are.

MORDECAI RICHLER:

Meanwhile, love, except as comic relief, between a short fat man and a flat-chested girl is still beyond the limits of the movies.

ARTHUR SCHLESINGER, JR.:

The Hollywood writer, like the radio writer and the pulp-fiction writer, tends to have a pervading sense of guilt.

GEORGE BERNARD SHAW:

Films bore me because they show interminable people getting in and out of limousines, trains, and buses. I am not interested in how people get to different places, but what they do when they get there.

ROBERT E. SHERWOOD:

The camera angles throughout afford an excellent and uninterrupted view of the heroine's nostrils.

JOHN STEINBECK:

Don't bother about me. The Grapes of Wrath *is unimportant compared to Shirley Temple's tooth.*

DYLAN THOMAS:

We watch the show of shadows kiss or kill. . . .

I'm not at all sure that I want such a thing, myself, as a poetic film. I think films fine as they are, if only they were better!

JAMES THURBER:

I will personally undertake to thrash anyone who mangles the dreams. They are wonderful. . . .

LEO TOLSTOY:
> I am seriously thinking of writing a play for the screen.

HAROLD TOWN:
> Film is a kind of shared universal memory as imperfect in this its natural effective state as the private memories of a childhood picnic.

> In crowds you pass by a random bit of Gable, just a moustache maybe, or a touch of Crawford in the imperious purpose of a lady's walk. I've seen the echo of Bette Davis at parties during a guest's virtuoso manipulation of a cigarette...the impatient lighting, the deep inhale, the upward glance, one arm cradling the other.

> But my eyes had turned inward to the dark where memories of the bejewelled Roxy swam, spewing the ambergris of Scheherazade dreams.

PAUL VALÉRY:
> I conceive of the cinema as an external memory endowed with mechanical perfection.

JOHN VAN DRUTEN:
> Romance in moving pictures? They have to meet cute.

EVELYN WAUGH:
> What is it about being on a boat that makes everyone behave like a film star?

ELIE WIESEL:
> One written sentence is worth eight hundred hours of film.

FRANZ WERFEL:
> It is undoubtedly the sterile reproduction of the external world with its streets, interiors, railway stations, restaurants, cars and beaches that has so far impeded the rise of film to the realm of art.

THORNTON WILDER:
> We'll trot down to the movies and see how girls with wax faces live.

THINKERS AND THEORISTS

DIANE ARBUS:
> It's always seemed to me that photography tends to deal with facts whereas film tends to deal with fiction.

BELA BALAZS:
> Man has again become visible.

IRIS BARRY:
> The film is a machine for seeing more than meets the eye.

ANDRÉ BAZIN:

Five years in the history of the cinema is easily the equivalent of a generation in literature.

ROLAND CAILLOIS:

There is no Cosmos on the screen, but an earth, trees, the sky, streets and railways: in short, matter.

NICOLA CHIAROMONTE:

The eye of the camera gives us that extraordinary thing: the world disinfected of consciousness.

RAYMOND DURGNAT:

Movie glamor is part of the artistic urge which tends, not towards the real, but towards the ideal. It is the Platonism of l'homme moyen sensuel, *for whom "heaven" is more Garden of Eden than a cloudy realm of sexless angels.*

RICHARD GRIFFITH:

To sit in the dark and behold a beauty that embodies all the dreams of men since time began is something new under the sun, and wonderful. If the movie camera needed justification, perhaps this is it.

CARL JUNG:

The cinema, like the detective story, makes it possible to experience without danger all the excitement, passion and desirousness which must be repressed in a humanitarian ordering of life.

NAIM KATTAN:

The photo of a film star leads, not to sensual joy with a living woman, but to another photo of another star, more daring and provocative than the first.

ARTHUR KNIGHT:

The film is really built and timed for audience reaction. I can't think of anything more deadly than seeing a comedy or even a Hitchcock thriller in an empty room.

SIEGFRIED KRACAUER:

The moviegoer watches the images on the screen in a dream-like state. . .the film screen is Athena's polished shield.

Film renders visible what we did not, or perhaps even could not see, before its advent.

SUSANNE K. LANGER:

The "dreamed reality" on the screen can move forward and backward because it is really an external and ubiquitous virtual present. . .the dream mode is an endless Now.

MARSHALL McLUHAN:

The movie is not only a supreme expression of mechanism, but, paradoxically, it offers as product the most magical of consumer commodities, namely dreams.

Movies as a nonverbal form of experience are like photography, a form of statement without syntax.

JONAS MEKAS:

Old Cinema, even when it is successful, is horrible; New Cinema, even when it fails, is beautiful.

If we study the modern film poetry, we find that even the mistakes, the out-of-focus shots, the shaky shots, the unsure steps, the hesitant movements, the over-exposed, the under-exposed bits, have become part of the new cinema vocabulary, being part of the psychological and visual reality of modern man.

ERWIN PANOFSKY:

The problem is to manipulate and shoot unstylized reality in such a way that the result has style.

HORTENSE POWDERMAKER:

In Hollywood, primitive magical thinking exists side by side with the most advanced technology.

SIR HERBERT READ:

Sculpture is the art of space, as music is of time. The film is the art of space-time: it is a space-time continuum.

Montage is mechanized imagination.

PAUL ROTHA:

The film is fundamentally an art based on observation.

GILBERT SELDES:

The movie is the imagination of mankind in action.

ROBERT WARSHOW:

I have gone to the movies constantly and, at times, almost compulsively for most of my life. I should be embarrassed to attempt an estimate of how many movies I have seen and how many hours they have consumed.

CRITICS AND INNOCENT BYSTANDERS

FRANKLIN PIERCE ADAMS:

Speaking of screen stars, there's a mosquito.

JAMES AGATE:

The theater, which talks about things rather than shows them, necessarily calls for a certain amount of imagination on the part of the playgoer, whereas the film, by showing everything, calls for no imagination at all.

ALEX BARRIS:

There's an old story about a Hollywood school child (in the days when the children of movie stars went to schools in Hollywood) who was instructed to write an essay on poverty. "Once upon a time," this moppet wrote, "there was a very poor family. The father was poor, and the mother was poor. The butler was poor, the maid was poor, the chauffeur was poor, and the gardeners were poor."

DICK CAVETT:

Movies are full of people who project a mysterious something on the screen that is entirely absent when you meet them.

JUDITH CRIST:

To be a critic, you have to have maybe three per cent education, five per cent intelligence, two per cent style, and ninety per cent gall and egomania in equal parts.

ST. JOHN ERVINE:

American motion pictures are written by the half-educated for the half-witted.

MANNY FARBER:

What we have, then, is a schizoid situation that can destroy the best actor: he must stay alive as a character while preserving the film's contrived style.

DAVID FROST:

The first words of film criticism I ever heard were "terrific" and "great."

ROBERT FULFORD:

The movie subtitle is such a powerful force in world culture that it's surprising how little serious attention it gets...people who like dubbing better than subtitling are not necessarily altogether evil.

WOLCOTT GIBBS:

It is my indignant opinion that ninety per cent of the moving pictures exhibited in America are so vulgar, witless, and dull that it is preposterous to write about them in any publication not intended to be read while chewing gum.

EZRA GOODMAN:

Movies and TV hope to be married, after which the happy bride and groom plan to raise a large family of slot machines.

SHEILAH GRAHAM, on Hollywood:
> *You could have everything, but it was nothing.*

RICHARD GRIFFITH, on stardom:
> *Five years was the standard stellar term, a ten-year star was a phenomenon, and we had to reach into Latin to describe someone who lasted longer than that—rara avis, sui generis.*

LEO GUILD, "the Wizard of Odds":
> *Gad! But Hollywood is a godly town! It's 7 to 3 if you live there you have never been divorced, and 2 in 19 you have never been drunk, and 3 to 10 you don't smoke.*

> *Benito Mussolini was paid two dollars a day in Rome for playing an extra in Sam Goldwyn's The Eternal City; Leon Trotsky made three dollars a day (in 1915) when he played in Rasputin at Fort Lee, New Jersey; the Duchess of Windsor, then known as Wallis Simpson, is reported to have drawn down five dollars from extra work in many pictures in Hollywood.*

MOLLY HASKELL:
> *Where are the women to create new fictions, to go beyond the inner space—as women are doing every day in real life—into the outer world of invention, action, imagination?*

> *There are two cinemas: the films we have actually seen and the memories we have of them.*

BJARNE HENNING-JENSEN:
> *And the critics would cry: "Can films be elevated only by the brassiere?"*

HEDDA HOPPER:
> *Nobody's interested in sweetness and light.*

> *For the first time in my life I envied my feet—they were asleep.*

> *I can wear a hat or take it off, but either way it's a conversation piece.*

> *Two of the cruelest, most primitive punishments our town deals out to those who fall from favor are the empty mail-box and the silent telephone.*

> *I can see it in print: The Truth, by Hedda Hopper, The Mad Hatter of Hollywood.*

PAULINE KAEL:
> *Is there a cure for film criticism?*

> *If debased art is kitsch, perhaps kitsch redeemed by honest vulgarity may become art.*

> *If somewhere in the Hollywood entertainment-world someone has*

managed to break through with something that speaks to you, then it isn't all corruption.

Movies are so rarely great art that if we cannot appreciate great trash we have very little reason to be interested in them.

ARTHUR KNIGHT:

Ordinarily when I review a film, I see it only once. But there are films that require going back to, and then, if possible, I do it.

Over the years, the movies have furnished America with its nearest equivalent to Europe's royalty.

JOHN KOBAL:

The last word on the film [Rita Hayworth's Salome (1953)] belongs to my local radio announcer, who confused the Judean Princess with a delicatessen. After finishing the evening news, he launched into the adverts, and entreated us to "Go and see Rita Hayworth's Salami. . . it'll take your breath away!"

C.A. LEJEUNE:

There are snake dances, sacrifices, private swimming baths, a Holy Mountain. The Mountain, by the way, has the privilege of belching when it is dissatisfied, something that the well-bred critic must not do.

Extensive tour
Of D. Lamour,
Nearly all
Of Jon Hall.
Sudden panic,
Cause volcanic,
And a torso
Or so.

DWIGHT MacDONALD:

About once a year—sometimes not so often—Hollywood turns out a movie that can be accepted without innumerable reservations.

WILSON MIZNER:

Over in Hollywood they almost made a great picture, but they caught it in time.

Some of the greatest love affairs I've known involved one actor, unassisted.

Always treat a lady like a woman and a woman like a lady.

GEORGE JEAN NATHAN:

Upon a well-tuned, well-trained, and sensitive mind the movies leave no impression other than one of having spent an hour or so in a spiritual vacuum.

LOUELLA PARSONS:
> Any dirt?

Sam Goldwyn, complained:
> Louella is stronger than Samson. He needed two columns to bring the house down. Louella can do it with one.

GERALD PRATLEY:
> A generation has come to know the cinema without having any first-hand knowledge of "glamour and stardom"—the quality which made it so exciting for their parents.

JAMES R. QUIRK:
> Photoplay readers were singularly calm in face of the news that Mary Pickford had bobbed her curls.

REX REED:
> If I have any philosophy at all, it's cancel the moon, turn off the klieg lights, and tell it like it is.

Ava Gardner observed about Reed:

> Rex Reed is either at your feet or at your throat.

CARROLL RIGHTER:
> Gable! Swanson! Crawford! There was glamor.

MARJORIE ROSEN:
> For the Cinema Woman is a Popcorn Venus, a delectable but insubstantial hybrid of cultural distortions.

DAVID SLAVITT:
> Mention Carmen Miranda in a serious way to a lot of intellectuals, and you're a genius. But mention Jeanne Moreau in a serious way, and you've said something merely banal and obvious.

RICHARD SCHICKEL:
> A movie star is not an artist, he is an art object.

> The frozen moment, the moment you can hold in your hands and study (and fantasize about at leisure) is often not only less perishable but more intense than the flowing moment, which is something your more impassioned cinemaddict tends either not to know or to have forgotten.

> It is the business of art to expand consciousness, while it is the business of mass communication to reduce it.

JACK SMITH:
> Film critics are writers, and they are hostile and uneasy in the presence of a visual phenomenon.

GLORIA STEINEM:

> *Writers in or out of Hollywood should be warned that they can no longer build plots on loss of virginity or fainting pregnant heroines and expect to be believed.*

DEEMS TAYLOR:

> *The picture was so expensive that only a box-office miracle could have made it profitable. The miracle did not occur.*

EARLE WILSON:

> *Actresses have busy minds. They're always changing them.*

> *A movie without sex would be like a candy bar without nuts in it.*

MAURICE ZOLOTOW:

> *When you are out there showing your dreams in public, your dreams have to be loved.*

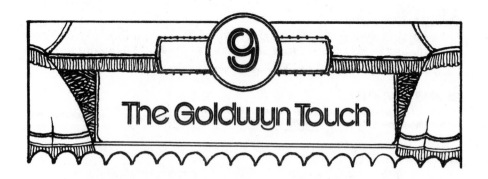

The Goldwyn Touch

"They keep watching my mouth all the time," Sam Goldwyn complained, "expecting something funny to pop out." Chances are something funny would pop out—a Goldwynism.

The creator of these hilarious malapropisms, Samuel Goldwyn (1884-1974), was Hollywood's leading independent film producer for thirty-five years. Born in Poland and brought to the United States at the age of eleven, he may have experienced some troubles with the English language but they did not impede his early career in the era of silent pictures.

He co-produced *The Squaw Man* (1913) and began independent production in 1924. Among his outstanding motion pictures are: *Arrowsmith* (1931), *Wuthering Heights* (1939), *The Best Years of Our Lives* (1946), *Guys and Dolls* (1955), and *Porgy and Bess* (1959). He placed a premium on production values, promotion, and his inimitable style—"the Goldwyn touch."

As for the authorship of the Goldwynisms, Clyde Gilmour, the film critic, once asked him, "Did you make them all up yourself?" The producer replied, "Some I did, and some I didn't. Who argues?" On another occasion he told an interviewer who inquired about them: "Goldwynisms! Don't talk to me about Goldwynisms. You want to hear some Goldwynisms, go talk to Jesse Lasky!"

WOE IS ME

Anyone who sees a psychiatrist should have his head examined.

I tell you, Marion, you just don't realize what life is all about until you've found yourself lying on the brink of a great abscess!

It's a goddamn sight easier to climb up a greased pole than to stay there!

If I did that I would be sticking my head in a moose.

He treats me like the dirt under my feet.

I've been laid up with intentional flu.

It's a dog-eat-dog world, and nobody's going to eat me.

The only thing left to go wrong on this picture is for me to go to jail.

SAM
GOLDWYN

THE GREAT I AM

I love the ground I walk on.

You may include me out.

For years I have been known for saying, "Include me out"; but today I am giving it up forever.

I can only express myself in two words: de-lighted.

In two words: im-possible.

I'll give you a definite maybe.

I had a monumental idea last night, but this morning I didn't like it.

Don't you hear me keeping still?

I'm exhausted from not talking.

I'm never going to write my autobiography as long as I live.

Ah, to be immortal for a day!

STARS

God makes the stars. It's up to the producers to find them.

I create stars, others make comets.

Actors think with their hearts. That's why so many of them die broke.

I'm having more trouble with these stars than Mussolini with Utopia.

She's pregnant? You know what you did? You didn't just screw her—you screwed me!

I'm overpaying Fredric March, but he's worth it.

Marion Davies is by far the most attractive of those stars who are not really eighteen.

The most important thing in acting is honesty; once you learn to fake that, you're in!

PERSONALITIES

Garson, you're a very clever genius.

You're a dunce who lived by the sweat of his Frau. [To an actor married to a German woman.]

Bill, you and I should start doing each other favors . . . let's start by you doing me one.

Norma, the way you play that part you should never make another picture!

Anita, you've got to cohabit with the director more.

Cheer up, Freddie. You've got the best part in the picture. . .and you, Anna, you've got the best part, too!

I apologize for calling you a crook, Doug. I can't prove it.

I'll cable Hitler and ask him to shoot around you. [To David Niven when he enlisted.]

PRODUCERS

Why only twelve at the Last Supper? That's the original number? Well, go out and get a supporting staff of thousands.

If you think you're not getting a fair deal, come to me and I'll prove how wrong you are.

All right, if you won't give me your word of honor, will you give me your promise?

A verbal contract isn't worth the paper it's written on.

Ars Gratia Artis. . .Art is Beholden to the Artists!

We can get all the Indians we need right at the reservoir.

Listen to me. We've got twenty-five years worth of files out there, just sitting around. Now what I want you to do is to go out there and throw everthing out—but make a copy of everything first!

A producer shouldn't get ulcers; he should give them.

Call me up tomorrow morning and remind me.

DIRECTORS

Most directors bite the hand that lays the golden egg.

The scene is too dull; tell him to put more life into his dying.

Elevate those guns a little lower.

All right, I'm a fair man. I'll submit anything to arbitration. But remember, no matter what's decided, McGuire goes to work for me!

This is it. You're fired. You're fired. Definitely. Wait a minute. I didn't say positively.

SCREEN WRITERS

This story is wonderful. It's magnificent. It's prolific!

This book has too much plot and not enough story.

The dictionary is nothing but a lot of words.

I want you to meet these two. Say hello to my favorite writers, Ken Englander and Everett What's-His-Name.

I've been paying him $5,000 a week for seven years, and you're trying to tell me his name?

I read part of it all the way through.

I've never seen so many unhappy people getting a hundred thousand dollars a year.

I ran into Howard Dietz last night. He was having dinner at my house.

Maurice Maeterlinck will get equal treatment with Rex Beach.

My God, the hero is a bee!

Don't worry, Mr. Maeterlinck, you'll make good yet.

I want to discuss the scene where the detective is marooning about on the lawn keeping his virgil.

Funny up the dreams.

She's a Lesbian? We'll get around that. We'll make her an American.

Too caustic? To hell with the cost; we'll make the picture anyway.

Let's have some new clichés.

Here I am paying big money to you writers and what for? All you do is change the words!

Let's bring it up to date with some snappy nineteenth-century dialog.

Disgusting! Disgusting! But how wonderful for my picture!

SPECIAL EFFECTS

There's not enough sarcasm in the musical score.

I want to hear it in two-by-four time.

You call that makeup? I call it breakup.

A wide screen just makes a bad film twice as bad.

MONEY

My God, you're going to sit there and tell me you care what somebody thinks when you make twenty times more than he does?

The banks can't afford me.

We put the money in the escarole.

I want this to be fifty-fifty like I said. But I want you to see that I get the best part of it.

I've found a backer. He wants us to meet him with a prospectus. What's a prospectus?

I know you're getting nothing, but I won't pay you a cent more.

I'll write you a blanket check.

To get what I want, I pay as much as I have to and as little as I can get away with.

Spare no expense to make everything as economical as possible.

The sweetness of low budget never equals the bitterness of low quality.

Why should people go out and pay money to see bad films when they can stay home and see bad television for nothing?

REFRESHMENTS

Send in two cups of demi-tasses.

No thanks. Coffee isn't my cup of tea.

Excuse me, I'm going out for some tea and trumpets.

Eat your vichyssoise before it gets cold.

Modern dancing is so old-fashioned.

The third baseman gets that? I wouldn't pay that much to a first baseman.

All the lies they tell about me are true.

I want something big enough and loud enough looking to be heard from the silent screen. And something that will scare off anything trying to steal our product...Leo the Lion!

Gentlemen, I've invented a new slogan—"Goldwyn Pictures Griddle the Earth."

What we've been having is "the best years of our lives."

The public is smarter than we are!

The press doesn't quote the twinkle in my eye.

I have nothing to say and what's more I won't say it until I get to New York.

Show me later.

CRITICS

I want you to know that a Goldwyn comedy is not to be laughed at.

Tell me, how did you love the picture?

Don't pay any attention to the critics—don't even ignore them.

FLOPS

The trouble with this business is the dearth of bad pictures.

If Roosevelt were alive today, he'd turn over in his grave.

Go see it and see for yourself why you shouldn't go see it.

When it comes to ruining a painting, he's an artist.

It's more than magnificent—it's mediocre.

Tomorrow we shoot, whether it rains, whether it snows, whether it stinks.

I am sorry that you felt the movie was too bloody and thirsty.

From quiet conferences come quiet pictures.

Usually when people are happy making a picture, it's a flop.

SMASH SUCCESS

If I don't say it's bad, it's good.

Excellent, but the next one must be better.

I was very pleasantly disappointed.

I don't care if it doesn't make a nickel. I just want every man, woman and child in America to see it.

Well, this preview was the greatest. They cheered for thirty minutes. Without stopping. We can fix it!

Are they going to like you in the next one?

MISPLACED MODIFIERS

It's spreading like wildflowers!

1810? When was that?

A sundial? What'll they think of next?

It's a century old, isn't it? Fifty years is a long, long time.

I never put on a pair of shoes until I've worn them at least five years.

I want that you should make a bust of my wife's hands.

My wife Frances is the best man I have.

That atomic bomb—it's dynamite.

You're from Iowa? Out here we pronounce it Ohio.

Why call your son Arthur? Every Tom, Dick, and Harry is called Arthur!

SLIPS OF THE TONGUE

He has warmth and charmth.

Anything that man says you've got to take with a dose of salts.

First you have a good story, then a good treatment, and next a first-rate director. After that, you hire a competent cast and even then you have only the mucus of a good picture.

It rolls off my back like a duck.

I'm glad we have with us tonight Marshall Field Montgomery.

Somebody should do a picture about the Russian Secret Police. You know, the GOP.

He worked his way up from nothing, that kid. In fact, he was born in an orphan asylum.

Our new executive was born in an orpheum asylum.

We have all passed a lot of water since then.

Plenty of water's passed between us.

My horse was in the lead, coming down the homestretch, when the caddy had to fall off.

Color television! Bah, I won't believe it until I see it in black and white.

I don't remember where I got this new Picasso. In Paris. Somewhere over there on the Left Wing.

That's my Toujours Lautrec.

PUBLICITY

People say that whenever I have a picture coming out I always start a controversy about something that gets into the papers. Well, in all sincerity, I want to assure you that as a general proposition—there's not a single word of untruth in that.

"The directorial skill of Mamoulian, the radiance of Anna Sten and the genius of Goldwyn have united to make the world's greatest entertainment." That is the kind of ad I like. Facts. No exaggeration.

You can see a motion picture any old time! Goldwyn is worth seeing all the time!

Isn't there a statue of limitation?

It's no use. You've got to take the bull between the teeth.

What a wonderful way to spend Sunday!

CLOSE-UPS

Sam has class.— Fred Astaire

You always knew where you stood with Sam Goldwyn: nowhere.— F. Scott Fitzgerald

I saw this empty taxicab drive up and out stepped Sam Goldwyn.— Sid Grauman

Inarticulate but stimulating. He filled the room with a wonderful panic and beat at your mind like a man in front of a slot machine, shaking it for a jackpot.— Ben Hecht

To understand Sam you must realize that he regards himself as a nation.— Lillian Hellman

A man of almost complete artistic integrity.— Alva Johnston

Sam Goldwyn was his own greatest production.— Richard Schickel

I'm afraid we will not get together, Mr. Goldwyn. You are interested in art, and I am interested in business.— George Bernard Shaw, as given by Howard Dietz in *Dancing in the Dark* (1974)

Sam Goldwyn created a caricature of himself and then wore it as a disguise.— Benjamin Sonnenberg

Short Subjects

Going to the movies, attending the Saturday matinees, was among the few rituals of my childhood, and certainly the most enjoyable. During the Forties, ten cents got me into the Century Theatre in downtown Kitchener, the small industrial city in Ontario in which I was born. Waiting in the block-long line in front of the ticket-seller simply increased my appetite, once inside, for the box of popcorn I would buy for five cents, and for the delights I would see on the immense screen, once I found myself a seat next to my chums.

What visual and voluble delights played the Century Theatre! Two and a half hours of them. There were two features (both B movies, action double bill), starring perhaps Gene Autry and Roy Rogers ("Which one is the King of the Cowboys?" asked the poster). Then there were three cartoons (a Bugs Bunny if we were lucky that week) and the umpteenth episode in a seemingly endless serial (perhaps Linda Sterling playing *The Tiger Woman*; this was in lieu of the compulsory newsreel, say *The March of Time*, which would play at the Lyric Theatre, the first-run house not too far away). But best of all was the trailer (the coming attractions were so exciting they guaranteed our presence at the Century Theatre every Saturday, rain or shine, school year, summer holidays, no matter). How much more exciting for the young moviegoer was this early experience to the later one of watching the same B movies and cartoons on television. How much more thrilling than today's movie-going experience of visiting a first-run house and seeing little more than a feature film—perhaps a trailer—and a "No Smoking" clip.

The above is meant as an introduction to what's below. "Short Subjects" brings together clips and takes that might otherwise be lost, thereby creating a sense of the confusion, clutter and excitement projected on the Century Theatre's screen, before it was torn down in the mid-Fifties, a casualty of that new invention, television. "Extra Takes" offers the reader some candid comments on well-known stars by known and lesser-known personalities. "Selected Shorts" presents a few often-overlooked features of the films. "Light on Dark" glances at censorship and "Un-American Activities," possibly, the dark side of the screen, solemn subjects lightly treated through quotation. "The Silents Speak" returns to the beginnings with lines—witty, wistful, sometimes prophetic, occasionally ironic—from some of the greats of the very early days. "Selling Yourselves" takes a short look at film promotion—sometimes called ballyhooey.

EXTRA TAKES

INGRID BERGMAN
"Say," went a joke in New York in 1945, "today I saw a picture without Ingrid Bergman in it." — David Shipman

CLARA BOW
There are few people in the world who possess IT. The only ones in Hollywood who do are Rex the wild stallion star, Spanish actor Tony Moreno, the Ambassador Hotel doorman, and Clara Bow.

— Elinor Glyn

She danced even when her feet were not moving. Some part of her was in motion in all her waking moments—if only her great rolling eyes. — Adolph Zukor

RICHARD BURTON
Make up your mind, Richard Burton. A household word or a great actor. — Sir Laurence Olivier

JAMES CAGNEY
James Cagney rolled through the film like a very belligerent barrel. — Noël Coward

MONTGOMERY CLIFT
Montgomery Clift is the only person I know who is in worse shape than I am. — Elizabeth Taylor

CLAUDETTE COLBERT
How would you like to play the wickedest woman in the world? — Cecil B. DeMille, casting the star as Cleopatra

TONY CURTIS
The trouble with Tony Curtis is that he's interested only in tight pants and wide billing. — Billy Wilder

MARION DAVIES
Marion Davies was one of the most delightfully accomplished comediennes in the whole history of the screen. She would have been a star if Hearst had never happened. — Orson Welles, on the influence of publisher William Randolph Hearst on the career of Marion Davies.

He took a beautiful, warm-hearted girl and made her the best-known kept woman in America and the butt of an infinity of dirty jokes, and he did it out of love and the blindness of love. — Pauline Kael

SAMMY DAVIS, JR.
Forty years ago there was a young Jewish entertainer named Al Jolson who was trying to pass as Negro. Today there is a young Negro entertainer named Sammy Davis who is trying to pass as Jewish. — Goodman Ace

DORIS DAY

Doris Day is as wholesome as a bowl of cornflakes and at least as sexy. — Dwight MacDonald

I've been around so long, I knew Doris Day before she was a virgin. — Groucho Marx

ERROL FLYNN

Errol Flynn says he doesn't worry about money—as long as he can reconcile his gross habits with his net income. — Sheilah Graham

JANE FONDA

Today's heroines are all like Jane Fonda. — Anita Loos

LILLIAN GISH

The movies have never known a more dedicated artist than Lillian Gish. — King Vidor

REX HARRISON

If, next to me, Rex Harrison were not the funniest light comedy actor in the world, he'd be good for only one thing: selling cars in Great Portland Street. — Noël Coward

AUDREY HEPBURN

Writing about Audrey Hepburn is like trying to wrap up 115 pounds of smoke. — Peter Martin

After so many drive-in waitresses in movies, here is class, someone who went to school, can spell and possibly play the piano...this girl singlehanded may make bozooms a thing of the past. — Billy Wilder

VAN JOHNSON

Van Johnson does his best: appears. — C.A. Lejeune

AL JOLSON

Al Jolson was a great instinctive artist with magic and vitality...he personified the poetry of Broadway, its vitality and vulgarity, its aims and dreams. — Charles Chaplin

ALAN LADD

Alan Ladd is hard, bitter and occasionally charming, but he is, after all, a small boy's idea of a tough guy. — Raymond Chandler

BURT LANCASTER

There are people who can't tell margarine from butter, and there are people who can't tell Kirk Douglas from Burt Lancaster. It's odd, because they're not really very much alike. — David Shipman

Burt Lancaster! Before he can pick up an ashtray, he discusses his motivation for an hour or two. You want to say, "Just pick up the ashtray, and shut up!" — Jeanne Moreau

CHARLES LAUGHTON

The well from which a man draws his talents is deep, but Laughton's well had no bottom. — Josef von Sternberg

OSCAR LEVANT

There's nothing wrong with Oscar Levant that a really first-class miracle couldn't cure. — Sam Behrman

JAYNE MANSFIELD

This country knows more about Jayne's statistics than the Second Commandment. — Billy Graham

POLA NEGRI

Pola Negri had a blind and uncritical admiration of her own genius in the blaze of which her sense of humor evaporated like a dew-drop on a million-watt arc lamp. — Rodney Ackland

KIM NOVAK

Kim Novak has a cute habit of getting herself set for a still picture, and, at the last minute, she unbuttons one more button in her cleavage. — George Lait

RIN-TIN-TIN

Rin-Tin-Tin had his own valet and chef, and his private limousine and chauffeur. — Joel Sayre

You survive bad pictures. Look at Rin-Tin-Tin. — Robert Mitchum

ROSALIND RUSSELL

I have a feeling God woke up Sunday and said, "You'd better send for Roz. She's suffered enough." — Frank Sinatra

JILL ST. JOHN

I'm thinking of going into the movies. I've got the connections now. — Henry Kissinger, who frequently escorted the lovely actress

OMAR SHARIF

Was that Omar Sharif riding the camel down Ventura last night? It was the one with the bumper sticker that says "Golda Meir is a shiksa." — Hal Kanter

NORMA SHEARER

Only a cloak stands between Norma Shearer and the fate thought to be worse than death but sometimes considered better than starving. — Richard Griffith

BARBARA STANWYCK

For twenty years I haven't stepped on a stage, or in front of a camera, without wearing the St. Genesius medal Barbara Stanwyck gave me. If he was the patron saint of actors, she, in my opinion, is the patroness. — Robert Preston

BARBRA STREISAND

I don't think there ever was a "Barbra the Terrible."— Peter Bogdanovich

JAMES STEWART

James Stewart is the most nearly normal of all Hollywood stars.— Louella Parsons

SHIRLEY TEMPLE

God made her just all by herself—no series. Just one.
— Bill "Bojangles" Robinson

RUDOLPH VALENTINO

I loved him not as one artist loves another, but as a woman loves a man.— Pola Negri

Rudolph Valentino was catnip to women.— H.L. Mencken

JOHNNY WEISSMULLER

Johnny Weissmuller would simply open his mouth, and the studio had a recording of three men, one a soprano, the other a baritone, and the third a hog caller, who yelled together. And that was the great Tarzan trademark.— Buster Crabbe

I cannot bring myself to prefer Lex Barker to Johnny Weissmuller, I cannot!— Frank O'Hara

RAQUEL WELCH

Raquel Welch is silicone from the knees up.— George Masters

ESTHER WILLIAMS

Esther Williams? Wet she is a star. Dry she ain't.— Fanny Brice

NATALIE WOOD

Natalie Wood is built like a brick dollhouse.— Harry Kurnitz

SELECTED SHORTS

ACADEMY AWARDS

Why, it looks like my Uncle Oscar!— Margaret Herrick, secretary to the American Academy of Motion Picture Arts and Sciences, on seeing the distinctive Award for the first time.

ANIMATION

I'm taking animation out of the nursery.— Ralph Bakshi, who introduced Fritz the Cat to the screen.

CASTING

You begin by choosing Ethel, John, and Lionel Barrymore, but by the time rehearsals start, you're grateful if your actors aren't albinos.— Emily Stevens

CINEMATOGRAPHY

A cameraman is often the chief in a film. His lighting can be the main factor in its success. — Lee Garmes

COSTUME DESIGN

Cary Grant and Grace Kelly. I guess they're my favorite pair.

— Edith Head

EXHIBITORS

Don't "Give the public what they want" — give 'em something better. — Samuel Lionel Rothafel, owner of Radio City Music Hall.

MAKE-UP

There'll always be a Westmore. — Frank Westmore

NEWSREELS

The last newsreel was laid out Wednesday night, and the old moviehouse staple has now gone the way of the fountain pen, the dirigible, and the dodo bird. — Richard F. Shepard

SHORT FEATURES

An exhibitor would no more think of omitting one or more shorts and a newsreel from his program than he would have kept his theater closed on New Year's Eve. — Pete Smith

LIGHT ON DARK

CENSORSHIP

Molly Haskell, critic:

The freedom that enables me not to go to porn films enables others to go.

Will H. Hayes, author of the Production Code:

I have sometimes thought that a part of the value I may have had for the industry was the fact, despite my long residence in New York, that I have somehow remained an unreconstructed Middle Westerner from "the sticks."

Joseph Wood Krutsch, literary critic:

The inanities blessed by Mr. Hayes are more genuinely corrupting than any pornography.

Jack Vizzard, movie watchdog:

Being a censor is like being a whore; everyone wants to know how you got into the business.

UN-AMERICAN ACTIVITIES

Edward Dmytryk, director, explaining himself:

When your country is in danger, you talk. That took more guts than remaining silent.

Eric A. Johnston, successor of Will H. Hayes, administrator of the Production Code:

The Communists hate and fear the American motion picture. It is their number one hate.

As long as I live, I will never be a party to anything as un-American as a blacklist.

John Howard Lawson, screen writer:

Today, when the American screen seems to have lost its ability to laugh, it is well to realize that there can be no comedy when fear or stupidity prevent recognition of the evils and absurdities that surround us.

Irving Thalberg, producer, to a friend about a mutual "blacklisted" friend:

There is no such thing as a blacklist. . . but I'll see that he gets off it.

Dalton Trumbo, screenwriter, who was one of the "Hollywood Ten":

The right to express ideas, good ideas, bad ideas, wicked ideas, crazy ideas, impossible ideas—this is the most precious right the individual can have.

It will do no good to search for villains or heroes because there were none. There were only victims.

Billy Wilder, acid-tongued director:

Only two of the Unfriendly Ten have talent. The rest are just unfriendly.

THE SILENTS SPEAK

Thomas Alva Edison, who gave "eyes" to motion pictures with his invention of the Kinetoscope, also gave "ears" to motion pictures with his refinement, the Kinetophonograph. This consisted of the primitive projector to which was added a synchronized cylinder gramophone. Difficulties with the latter delayed the development of sound. Even *The Jazz Singer*, which Warners released on October 6, 1927, was transitional: it was essentially a silent picture with musical accompaniment on a synchronized disc. But, once vocal, the films have never again been silent.

Let's listen to some of the stars of the silent eras. Some, like Valentino, typify the pre-1927 period. Others, like Swanson, suggest the transition into the post-1927 period. Most of them celebrated their palmy days on the screen and—"the rest is silence."

ROSCOE "FATTY" ARBUCKLE, involved in a 1921 sex scandal:
All I want is for the public to withhold its judgment until the jury of twelve men and women has decided whether or not I am guilty.

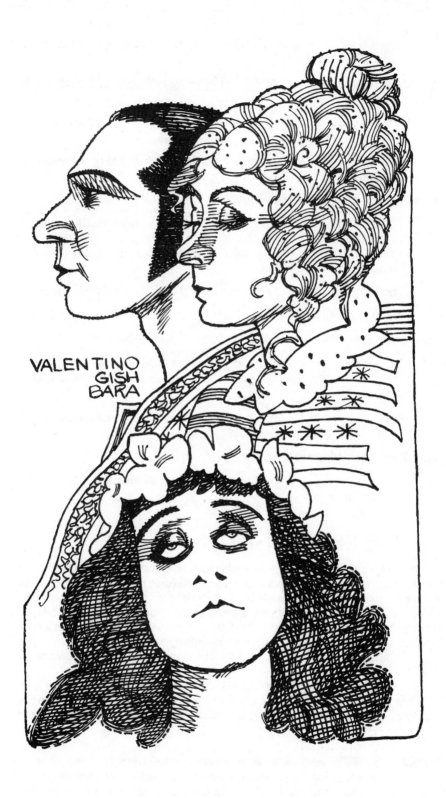

VALENTINO
GISH
BARA

THEDA BARA:

Never have I liked being a vampire and never, of course, have I believed there was any "such animal," and since the public did and liked to see me as one, I agreed to become one.

I'm going to continue doing vampires as long as people sin.

SARAH BERNHARDT, before her death in 1923:

I rely upon these films to make me immortal.

CLARA BOW:

We had individuality. We did as we pleased. We stayed up late. We dressed the way we wanted. I'd whiz down Sunset Boulevard in my open Kissel . . . with several red Chow dogs to match my hair. Today, they're sensible and end up with better health. But we had more fun.

Being a sex symbol is a heavy load to carry, especially when one is very tired, hurt and bewildered.

FRANCIS X. BUSHMAN:

I have no place to go but down.

LEW CODY:

A male vampire exists because all women want to be a man's last love, not his first.

DOLORES DEL RIO:

Nevair, nevair, will I make a talkie. I zink zey are tairibble.

So long as a woman has twinkles in her eyes, no man notices whether she has wrinkles under them.

MARIE DRESSLER:

I was born with a terrific urge to please people, to make them happy. Only when others are happy can I be happy too.

If ants are such busy workers, how come they find time to go to all the picnics?

JOHN GILBERT:

Lots of people live and die without ever knowing that one great love.

They can't ruin me with one bad talking picture!

LILLIAN GISH:

I think the things that are necessary in my profession are these: taste, talent, and tenacity. I think I have had a little of all three.

Oh, dear, I've got to go throught another day of kissing John Gilbert.

What makes a star? Necessity!

AL JOLSON:

In Hollywood I played poker with the film magnates. I played for about a minute because they regard ten thousand dollars as tissue paper.

ELMO LINCOLN:

In the old days I used to beat my chest like the apes. Now Tarzan yells with his hand cupped to his mouth.

I swung around in the trees eight feet above ground. There's nothing to it, providing you hold on and let go at the right time.

MAE MURRAY:

May I introduce myself? I'm Mae Murray, the young Ziegfeld beauty with the bee-stung lips—and Hollywood is calling me.

NITA NALDI:

We didn't have any censors in those days, but we did have our own bosoms and our own eyelashes...and we never took ourselves seriously.

ALLA NAZIMOVA:

Today I have not so many things, and I am happier.

POLA NEGRI:

Hollywood has gone from Pola to Polaroid.

RAMON NOVARRO:

Who wants pheasant under glass, stuffed squab, and those fancy salads when he can get a good beef stew? I like food that puts hair on your chest.

GLORIA SWANSON:

In those days they wanted us to live like kings. So we did—and why not? We were in love with life. We were making more money than we ever dreamed existed, and there was no reason to believe that it would ever stop.

I have gone through enough of being nobody. I have decided that, when I am a star, I will be every inch and every moment the star. Everyone from the studio gateman to the highest executive will know it.

The world is not what it was. There isn't a country that isn't worse than it used to be.

I don't know whether you're applauding my acting—or my age. I'll be seventy on my next birthday.

I really am the greatest star of them all.

My epitaph should read, "She paid all her bills."

BLANCHE SWEET:
I also did too much just for money. I was ashamed of myself, but I couldn't resist. Ten thousand dollars a week is awfully hard to resist.

CONSTANCE TALMADGE:
Leave them while you're looking good, and thank God for the trust funds Momma set up.

NORMA TALMADGE:
All things strike an unhappy balance in the end.

HELEN TWELVETREES:
I have no illusions about lasting fame.

RUDOLPH VALENTINO:
Heaven knows, I'm no sheik.

We cannot know woman because she does not know herself.

A love affair with a stupid woman is like a cold cup of coffee.

I am beginning to look more and more like my miserable imitators.

COME TO THE MOVIES

What follow are some wonderful campaigns conducted by movie studios to advertise themselves and their product. Hollywood ballyhoo has never been bettered, except by the unknown cynic who described an unproduced film in these words:

The book they said could never be written has become the movie they said could never be filmed!

Steve Broidy, a studio executive, once observed that the slogans and catchphrases were often superior to the films:

Why don't we put some sprocket-holes in the press-book and throw the picture away?

The film pioneer, Adolph Zukor, founded his own company, Famous Players, in 1912, and advertised it succinctly and aptly as:

Famous Players in Famous Plays.

Lewis J. Selznick, another pioneer, the father of David O. Selznick, established Selznick Select a few years later, creating the following slogan:

Selznick Pictures Make Happy Hours.

No one remembers who selected the Metro-Goldwyn-Mayer motto, "Ars Gratia Artis," the Latin for "Art for Art's Sake," but it was composer and MGM executive Howard Dietz who came up with its proud (and true enough) slogan:

More Stars Than There Are in Heaven.

In the 1950's, the same Dietz, then vice-president of the Council of Motion Picture Organizations, headed the "Movietime, USA" campaign to champion the motion picture arts against television. Although he does not claim the honors, he probably originated its catchy campaign slogan:

The Movies are Better than Ever.

SMASH HITS!

A Cast of 125,000!

Ben Hur (1927). This may well be the first appearance of the cliché "With a Cast of Thousands!"

Garbo Talks!

Anna Christie (1930), Greta Garbo's first talking picture. Authorship of the two words is attributed to Howard Dietz.

The strangest love a man has ever known!

Dracula (1931). Directed by Tod Browning.

Garbo Laughs!

Ninotchka (1939). Garbo plays light comedy. Howard Dietz at work again.

How would you like to tussel with Russell?

The Outlaw (1943). Starring Jane Russell. Attributed to Howard Hughes.

There never was a woman like Gilda!

Gilda (1946). Starring Rita Hayworth.

Gable's Back and Garson's Got Him.

Adventure (1945). Starring Greer Garson and Clark Gable just returned from the war. Howard Dietz wrote this one too.

Nobody's as good as Bette when she's bad.

Beyond the Forest (1949). Starring Bette Davis.

A Lion in Your Lap!

Bwana Devil (1953). The first 3D film, directed by Arch Oboler.

Don't pronounce it—see it!

Phffft (1954). Directed by Mark Robson.

God created woman, but the Devil created Brigitte Bardot.

184   *And God Created Woman* (1957). Directed by Roger Vadim.

The Birds Is Coming!

The Birds (1963). This clever line is attributed to the director Alfred Hitchcock.

The Motion Picture with Something to Offend Everyone!

The Loved One (1965). Based on Evelyn Waugh's caustic novel, and directed by Tony Richardson.

Pray for Rosemary's baby!

Rosemary's Baby (1968). Directed by Roman Polanski.

Love means never having to say you're sorry.

Love Story (1970). This is a key line from the novel by Eric Segal.

A long time ago in a galaxy far, far away. . . .

Star Wars (1977). Directed by George Lucas.

You'll believe a man can fly.

Superman: The Movie (1978). Directed by Richard Donner.

Movie Moments

Everyone cherishes a favorite motion-picture sequence, scene or shot, and re-screens it in memory long after its image has vanished from the silver screen. Why are memorable sequences so quickly forgotten, and silly ones impossible to forget? Why do gestures, situations, or words stand out? Why should a gauche line of dialogue bury itself in the memory, while a great one dissolves in the dark? There is no accounting for taste or for the tricks of memory. The cinematic highs—and lows—that follow have over the years been singled out for their memorability. They move audiences to extremes. Many of them are my favorite movie moments. I hope they are yours too.

Kiss me, my fool!

Well-remembered title in the silent movie *A Fool There Was* (1916), starring Theda Bara, the original vamp. "She was the first woman offered commercially, in movies, as an object of sexual fantasy." (David Thomson)

Lady Diana: Why have you brought me here?
Sheik Ahmed Ben Hassan: Are you not woman enough to know?

Widely quoted lines from E.M. Hull's novel *The Sheik* (1921), turned into a scandalously successful film starring Rudolph Valentino as the Sheik and Agnes Ayres as the woman he abducted. The title-cards of the movie enshrine some other gems. Lady Diana donned a man's outfit but this did not fool the Sheik: "You make a charming boy, but it was not a boy I saw in Biskra." Lady Diana finally succumbs to the Sheik's charms: "I am not afraid with your arms around me, Ahmed, my desert love, my sheik."

THE TAMING OF THE SHREW... With Mary Pickford and Douglas Fairbanks...By William Shakespeare... With Additional Dialogue by Sam Taylor.

Celebrated screen title and credits for *The Taming of the Shrew* (1928), which inadvertently placed Sam Taylor, an otherwise undistinguished screenwriter and the film's director as well, on a par with the Bard.

Wait a minute, wait a minute, you ain't heard nothin' yet, folks!

Al Jolson in *The Jazz Singer* (1927). With this line, said to be an ad lib, the era of silent pictures came to an end and sound held sway.

I'm sorry for everybody in the whole world.

Famous—and fatuous—line spoken by the actress Jeanne Eagels in *Sadie Thompson* (1928), the first movie version of the play *Rain* (1922), based on the short story by W. Somerset Maugham.

When you say that, smile:

Gary Cooper to Trampas, played by Walter Huston, in *The Virginian* (1930).

Excuse me while I slip into something more comfortable....

Jean Harlow, wearing an evening dress, to Ben Lyon in *Hell's Angels* (1930).

Mother of Mercy, is this the end of Rico?

Edward G. Robinson, the gangster, dying in a shoot-out, in *Little Caesar* (1930).

It's alive! It's alive! It's alive!

Colin Clive, as Dr. Frankenstein, at the birth of his monster, in *Frankenstein* (1931).

I never drink...wine.

Listen to them...children of the night...what music they make!

Bela Lugosi, as Count Dracula, on being offered a glass of wine, then drawing attention to the wolves' cries, in *Dracula* (1931).

You are all criminals because you want to be. But I...I do what I do because I can't help it!

Peter Lorre, as the child-murderer, pleading with his accusers, all criminals themselves, in Fritz Lang's *M* (1931).

It took more than one man to change my name to...Shanghai Lily.

Marlene Dietrich, as a woman of the world, to Clive Brook, one of the world's innocents, in *Shanghai Express* (1932).

Me Tarzan, you Jane.

Johnny Weissmuller, as Tarzan, to Maureen O'Sullivan, as Jane, in *Tarzan the Ape Man* (1932), written by Ivor Novello.

I vant to be left alone.

Greta Garbo, playing the reclusive artiste, in *Grand Hotel* (1932). She did not say, "I vant to be alone."

Grand Hotel...always the same...people coming, going...nothing ever happens.

Lewis Stone, doorman, standing in front of the swinging doors of *Grand Hotel* (1933).

Why don't you come up sometime...see me?

Mae West to Cary Grant in *She Done Him Wrong* (1933). Mae West wrote the script herself, and this is what she said, though the public remembers the invitation as "Come up and see me sometime."

Oh, no, it wasn't the aviators. It was beauty killed the beast.

Robert Armstrong as the foolhardy hunter Carl Denham in *King Kong* (1933).

We belong dead!

Boris Karloff, as Frankenstein, referring to his nearly-made "bride," Elsa Lanchester, in *The Bride of Frankenstein* (1935).

We have ways of making men talk.

Douglass Dumbrille, as Mohammed Khan, to a helpless prisoner in *Lives of a Bengal Lancer* (1935).

Come here, Mister Christian!

Charles Laughton, as Captain Bligh, summoning Clark Gable, as Fletcher Christian, in *Mutiny on the Bounty* (1935).

As the sun sinks over the horizon.... And so we leave beautiful—

James A. Fitzpatrick, writer, narrator, and producer of innumerable Fitzpatrick Traveltalks, short features popular in the 1930s and 1940s.

Time Marches On!

Westbrook Von Voorhis, "radio's most famous voice," narrating the monthly newsreel *The March of Time* (1935-51). Other over-dramatizers were Ted Husing and Harry Von Zell (who described the delivery as "similar to that of a teletype machine—crisp, flat").

What's up, Doc?... Of course you realize this means war.

Bugs Bunny, Warner Brothers' wisecracking rabbit, in any of the cartoons voiced by Mel Blanc since 1936.

The calla lilies are in bloom again....

Katharine Hepburn, playing an actress, in *Stage Door* (1937).

Every man carries in his heart a Shangri-La.

Whispered by the Grand Lama, played by Sam Jaffe, in *Lost Horizon* (1937).

Somewhere over the rainbow
Way up high
There's a land that I heard of
Once in a lullaby....

Judy Garland, as Dorothy, in *The Wizard of Oz* (1939). The words are by Harold Arlen, the music by E.Y. Harburg.

Frankly, my dear, I don't give a damn.

Clark Gable, as Rhett Butler, to Vivien Leigh, as Scarlett O'Hara, in *Gone With the Wind* (1939).

After all, tomorrow is another day.

Vivien Leigh, as Scarlett O'Hara, in *Gone With the Wind* (1939).

One doesn't easily forget, Herr Baron, an arm torn out by the roots.

Lionel Atwill as a police inspector to Basil Rathbone in *Son of Frankenstein* (1939).

Oliver: Here's another fine mess you've gotten me into.
Stan: We'll talk about it later, Olly.

Exchange between Stan Laurel and Oliver Hardy in almost any of a number of their features made in the 1930s and 1940s.

Last night I dreamed I went to Manderley again....

Joan Fontaine, off screen, beginning *Rebecca* (1940). Leslie Halliwell, the film historian, refers to this as "the most famous line in film history."

By gad, sir—I don't know what you'll say or do next, but whatever it is, it's bound to be extraordinary!

Sidney Greenstreet as "the fat man" to Humphrey Bogart playing Sam Spade in *The Maltese Falcon* (1941).

Rosebud.

Orson Welles, as Charles Foster Kane, dying words, in *Citizen Kane* (1941). Unquestionably, the most famous word in film history.

You played it for her, you can play it for me. If she can stand it, I can. Play it!

Humphrey Bogart to pianist Dooley Wilson, in *Casablanca* (1942). Bogart is referring to the tune "As Time Goes By." He did not say, "Play it again, Sam." Nor, for that matter, did Charles Boyer ever say, on film, "Meet me at the Casbah."

I'm hard to get—all you have to do is ask me.

If you want anything, just whistle....You know how to whistle, don't you, Steve? You just put your lips together...and blow.

Lauren Bacall to Humphrey Bogart in *To Have and Have Not* (1944).

Nobody gets the best of Fred C. Dobbs.

Humphrey Bogart playing the crazed prospector in *The Treasure of the Sierra Madre* (1948), directed by John Huston.

Look, Ma! Top of the world:

James Cagney, deliberately incinerating himself, in *White Heat* (1949).

In Switzerland they had brotherly love, five hundred years of democracy and peace, and what did they produce? The cuckoo clock!

Orson Welles, as Harry Lime, to Joseph Cotten, as Holly Martens, high above Vienna on the Prater ferris-wheel, in *The Third Man* (1949). Welles himself wrote these lines.

Fasten your seat belts. It's going to be a bumpy night.

Bette Davis, as an aging actress, to all and sundry at a cocktail party in *All About Eve* (1950), written and directed by Joseph L. Mankiewicz.

We didn't need dialog; we had faces then. They don't have faces any more—maybe one, Garbo.

This is my life—it always will be. All right, Mr. DeMille. I'm ready for my close-up!

Gloria Swanson (as the aging idol Norma Desmond) in *Sunset Boulevard* (1950).

I'm singin' in the rain,
Just singin' in the rain....

Gene Kelly, singing and dancing in a downpour, in the most popular of all musicals, *Singin' in the Rain* (1952), with words by Arthur Freed and music by Nacio Herb Brown.

She came at me in sections.

Fred Astaire speaking of Cyd Charisse in *The Band Wagon* (1953), written by Howard Dietz.

You've got that little something extra that Ellen Terry talked about....it's called "star quality."

James Mason to Judy Garland in *A Star is Born* (1954).

Love means never having to say you're sorry.

Ryan O'Neal to Ali McGraw, in *Love Story* (1970). Perhaps the most famous of fatuous lines. It comes from Eric Segal's bestselling novel of the same name.

We'll make him an offer he can't refuse.

Marlon Brando, playing the aged Don Vito Corleone, to Robert Duvall, playing the family lawyer, in *The Godfather* (1969), directed by Francis Ford Coppola.

May the Force be with you.

Alec Guinness, as Ben (Obi-Wan) Kenobi, the aged knight, to young Luke Skywalker, played by Mark Hamill, in *Star Wars* (1977).

I never drink when I fly.

Christopher Reeve, Superman, to Margot Kidder, Lois Lane, declining the glass of wine she has offered him, in *Superman: The Movie* (1978).

I'm trying to corner the last pea on my plate.

James Mason, as Dr. Watson, to Christopher Plummer, as Sherlock Holmes, while struggling to catch the last pea on his dinner plate, in *Murder by Decree* (1979).

TIA MAK

Final frames of *Nanook of the North* (1921), the first feature-length documentary, written and directed by Robert Flaherty. In Inuktituut (the Eskimo language), these two words mean: "The End."

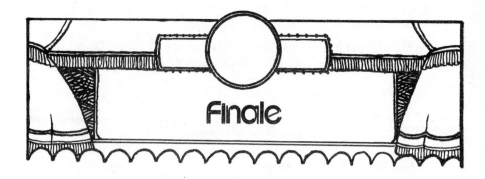

Finale

Film historian Ben M. Hall, author of *The Golden Age of the Movie Palace: The Best Remaining Seats* (1961), has reproduced the following notice which he says was written in language "simple yet worthy of a passage from Genesis." The notice dates from the silent days and was found backstage by the switchboard of the 850-seat Paradise Theater, Faribault, Minnesota:

> *PLEASE DO NOT TURN ON THE CLOUDS*
> *UNTIL THE SHOW STARTS.*
> *BE SURE THE STARS ARE TURNED OFF*
> *WHEN LEAVING.*

Hall himself has a gift for turning a phrase; he referred to the old-fashioned movie palace, that opulent temple to the cinematic muse, as "an acre of seats in a garden of dreams." He felt, suddenly, with the advent of sound, that much of the excitement, glamor, mystery, and beauty simply vanished from the scene. "There was popcorn in paradise," he later wrote.

Arthur Mayer, once said of the journeymen who assemble the motion pictures:

> *I'm always a little bit afraid of ART in big capital letters. All in all, the best work in Hollywood has been that of people who didn't regard themselves as artists in any sense of the word. They were craftsmen who had a job to do.*

He then satirized Hollywood hyperbole of the Forties using a phrase beloved of *Variety*:

> *It was merely colossal.*

Our closing lines come from the early days of film, from the baroque prose of Terry Ramsaye, historian of early film-making and author of *A Million and One Nights* (1926):

> *The genii had answered the Wish of the World with the Aladdin's Lamp of the camera and the Magic Carpet of the film. An empire built of shadow glories has prospered, and its boundaries are the limits of Earth.*
>
> *We, like Scheherazade, have come to the end of our tales.*